SO YOU WANT TO PLAY

WITH

PETER ALLISS

This 109-minute BBC video (BBCV 4867) gives a new look to the problems of playing the game for the everyday golfer. Informative, instructive and entertaining, it is designed to appeal to people of all ages and abilities, whether already playing or thinking of taking up the game. It is available from all good video stockists.

SO YOU WANT TO PLAY GOLF

WITH

PETER ALLISS

PETER ALLISS

WITH BOB FERRIER

BBC BOOKS

PICTURE CREDITS

Allsport 43, 117, 125; Cartoon Centre at University of Kent at
Canterbury, Courtesy the Estate of H.M. Bateman 112; Colorsport 63,
124; Peter Dazeley 20–21, 69, 89, 103; Hailey Sports Photography
46–48, 56; Hulton Deutsch Collection 100; Lawrence Levy/Yours In
Sport 81, 87; Mark Newcombe/Visions In Golf 36, 65, 90, 122;
Courtesy Oakland Hills Golf Club 109; Phil Sheldon 44, 55, 66–68,
70–73, 75, 84, 105–106, 111, 115–116, 121, 127, 128–130.

Location Photography Courtesy Walt Disney World.

With Special thanks to John Bodnar.

With thanks to Delta Air Lines and Walt Disney World

Published by BBC Books,
a division of BBC Enterprises Limited,
Woodlands, 80 Wood Lane
London W12 0TT

First Published 1993
© Peter Alliss and Bob Ferrier 1993
The moral rights of the authors have been asserted
ISBN 0 563 36902 7
Set in Monotype Perpetua by Goodfellow & Egan Ltd, Cambridge
Printed and bound in Great Britain by Butler & Tanner Ltd, Frome
Colour separations by Tecknik Ltd, Berkhamstead
Cover printed by Clays Ltd, St Ives Plc

CONTENTS

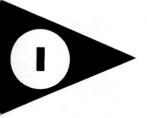

INTRODUCTION

When the BBC decided that it wanted another series of six golf programmes for television, producer John Bodnar and I felt that this one somehow should be different. The result of our discussions became *So You Want to Play Golf*. We felt that golf is such a multi-faceted game, and so unlike other games, that we should try to touch on its many facets, off the course as well as on, and also invoke a representation of the wide range of people who play it – young and old, men and women, amateur and professional. This ancient game is rich in many ways. It is simple, yet immensely complicated. The golf swing is entirely logical, yet so difficult to repeat. The playing of golf demands a lockerful and a wardrobeful of equipment. It requires teaching, learning, practice, then playing. It is not as cheap as football, which we can do with a ball and an open space. A golf course requires funding, land purchase, design and construction in the first place, and continuing maintenance thereafter.

The sheer concept of the golf club is almost a unique social entity. It has a major contribution to make to the social and cultural quality of the life of its town, district or region, not to mention its creature comforts of bar, restaurant and dressing rooms, and the fellowship such a club creates. The Rules of Golf are 34 in number and carry with them definitions and appendices that make the whole thing run to about 100 pages, which at first glance can be intimidating. A closer inspection will show, however, that there is little there which is superfluous, that these rules are expressed simply, carefully and above all realistically and logically and arise directly from the experiences of golfers in play. But some do remain complicated and hard to remember. We have tried to remedy this and you will find special sections throughout the book which feature explanations of the more demanding of them. The Rules of Golf are created, guarded, nurtured and amended by a joint committee of the Royal and Ancient Golf Club of St Andrews and of the United States Golf Association, which meets formally every four years and between times is in continuous communication. The game has been blessed with having men of probity on committees for more than half a century, men who are not financially rewarded in any way for their labours. The game is in good hands.

The televising of the great championships and competitions of golf has created a vast new public for the game, as it has done for other sports. The most beautiful courses in the world shown on television have brought to millions of people an awareness of the subtleties of golf course design and architecture, and the development of the home video has allowed them to have permanent records of great players and great events, all bringing golf tuition into the living room. The game as a result has grown enormously. When I was a young tournament professional, we had perhaps a dozen events to play for each year. The French Open was the outstanding event on the Continent, and going there, to these lovely, aristocratic courses, was a grand adventure, an introduction to food and drink and culture differing from our own. Now the PGA European Tour has an event, or events, almost every week and geographically ranges from Scandinavia to North Africa, through the Middle East to Thailand. In the fifties, the lucky ones among us might go to the United States every four years for Ryder Cup matches, making the ocean crossing by steamship! Now, playing in the US 10 or 15 times each year is routine for our best players, and travelling to Japan is not unusual for many.

We decided to make the television programmes in Florida, to

Golf in America is full of surprises, but golf at Disney World...? Nick Price, Harriet Rowe and Paula Sainty, can't quite believe Mickey and Peter and Goofy, but ...

7

escape the uncertainties of a British winter and to make the best use of the near-certainty of Florida sunshine. Our venue was the Walt Disney World Resort, near Orlando, a wondrous place covering some 45 square miles and including five and a half golf courses. To reveal some of the magic, some of the mysteries, of the game, we had the best coaches, men and women, that the US had to offer, and they came from far and wide. And we brought our pupils all the way from the UK, courtesy of Delta Air Lines, golfers young and old, men and women, low and high handicappers, a left-hander, a one-armed golfer, even a blind player – a complete cross-section of the democracy of our game. They all enjoyed themselves, they worked extremely hard, they learned a great deal about golf – and, I trust, about the rules, or those most often broken.

Perhaps the most thrilling of all our experiences at the Walt Disney World Resort was working with our disabled chums – Ron Allfree, the blind golfer, and Andy Robinson, the one-armed golfer – of course their problems were the problems of all golfers: the shoulders, the hips, the grip, the top of the backswing, following through. But their tenacity at getting their golfing problems sorted out was an example to us all.

It was not our intention to make this another 'How to . . .' television series. Our hope was to take a wider and deeper look at the game and some aspects of it which are not given enough consideration, or the right kind of consideration. This book is a companion to the television series, and I trust it reflects the diversity of golf which I believe we achieved in those programmes.

2 ▶ THE 'LEARNERS'

PAULA SAINTY

Paula Sainty – in her middle twenties, 5ft 5in tall and of slim build – is our 'absolute beginner'. More accurately she is a relative beginner in golf, having played seriously for less than a year. She first became aware of the game in her early teens when she used to accompany her father to a golf driving range at Watford, eventually saying, 'Dad, can I have a go?' Her father is an active 15-handicap golfer at the Porters Park club at Radlett, and Paula plays with him whenever possible. She hopes soon to join a club and establish a proper handicap; although she plays to around 28, her immediate ambition is simply to improve her game. She says that taking part in the series in Florida was 'fantastic – the chance of a lifetime'. It arose when John Bodnar, the producer of the series, was talking casually with Paula's boss (she works for BBC Videos) who said, 'Paula in my office might be interested in that.' She was!

Paula now believes that the experience helped her game substantially in general and, in particular, her bunker play and understanding of the swing.

BRYAN NICKLESS

Bryan Nickless, 45, is managing director of Talisman Communications, a company which provides media, publishing and communications services to major corporations. He was born in Birmingham, and business has taken him first to Manchester, more recently to London, and with that membership of the Woburn Golf and Country Club. Sport has been something of a way of life for Bryan. He played senior Rugby Football until he was 28. A business conference at the Peebles Hydro hotel in the Scottish Borders introduced him to golf, when he was invited to play on the local course. A left-hander, he played right-handed that day with borrowed clubs, but 'the weather was beautiful, the course was beautiful, the scenery was beautiful, and I thought I'd better investigate this remarkable game'. That one round did it.

He arranged for some lessons, became a member of Astbury Golf Club, near Congleton, and worked his handicap down to 14. In 1979, he moved to the London area, and was soon playing to a seven handicap. Pressure of business has meant it is now in the 10–11 range. To

join the BBC expedition to Florida took a 'good deal of juggling in re-arranging business'. At Walt Disney World Resort he was helped with 'a bit of bunker play and, in particular, putting – amateur players very seldom think of getting tuition in putting'. But being there was too good to miss, and his greatest pleasure was in watching his son Daniel 'playing and learning'.

DANIEL NICKLESS

Daniel Nickless, 16, was introduced to golf by his father, Bryan, when he was eight years old. When he was 11, his father arranged junior membership for him at the Woburn Golf and Country Club. Danny attends Vandyke Upper School at Leighton Buzzard and, like his father, he has always been very much into sport, playing cricket, rugby, basketball and football. He wants very much to become a tournament professional, and he went to Florida with BBC Television very much on that basis – as a young aspirant tournament pro. With a name like 'Nickless', one might think he has made a reasonable start down that road.

His Florida experience, he says, was invaluable in that he got important insights into the mental side of the game. 'Rina Ritson really knows the game, knows the golf swing, inside out,' he says. 'Wally Armstrong and Mr Alliss taught me a great deal about the mental side of the game, about concentration, about tactics, when to be defensive, when to be aggressive, and that there is a lot more to competitive golf than just hitting the ball. It's about understanding the whole game.'

HARRIET ROWE

Harriet Rowe's parents played golf at Woking, and as a result she grew up very much aware of the game and was a very early starter. She was a junior member of both Woking and Worplesdon golf clubs, both in that stretch of Surrey of heather and pine and sandy sub-soil which makes perfect ground for golf courses. Harriet remains a member at Woking. By her middle teens, she was six handicap and a member of the Surrey Girls team, being joined in time by such luminaries as Laura Davies and Sally Prosser. More recently, working as a BBC production secretary in London on television documentaries, her golfing time has been restricted, and her handicap increased to 15.

Reflecting on her Walt Disney World Resort experience, Harriet sees her work around the greens and her short game in general much improved, specifically her putting. Harriet felt that the bunker instruction was particularly helpful to all the 'students'. Much of the pleasure she gets from the game is from 'playing against myself'. Now she feels that she is getting her self-belief, her confidence, back to where it was when she left school some ten years ago, and she is planning to increase her golfing time as much as possible.

TERRY WHITE

When Terry White, 65, retired from Tesco five years ago, he was Director of Distribution for the national supermarket company and had had an exciting business life. Until he was 40, he had been a very active cricketer, playing in a high class of village cricket. He then started golf and became captain of Apsley Guise Golf Club in Bedfordshire, and is now on the committee of the Woburn Club, which he and his wife joined in 1981. He has a handicap of 14 and in retirement has had a few years of golfing leisure, having played fine courses in Spain, France, Italy, Ireland and Scotland.

In Florida, he felt that his chipping and pitching in particular were greatly improved. He was most impressed by the work of Donald Crawley, the exiled Yorkshireman who is now Director of Instruction at the John Jacobs Golf Schools, and was also completely fascinated by how television films are put together, with all the technicalities involved.

JOAN WHITE

Joan White, wife of Terry, is a lady of mature years (all right, let's say she has just turned 60), who found in golf a certain respite from years and years of organizing 'cricket teas' as her husband and his cronies indulged their first sporting love. She too has played golf for the past 20 years, but only regularly over the past ten, since she took early retirement from schoolteaching. With Terry, she joined Woburn in 1981 and now has a handicap of 23. She plays with Terry and friends at home and also on golfing holidays, and loves the game for the companionship it offers, and because it happens in the open air and can be played all year round.

Joan was thrilled by her Florida experience, by the quality of the courses and their facilities and above all by Rina Ritson, the head professional at the Walt Disney World Resort's Buena Vista course. Joan had been concerned for some time that she 'hadn't been hitting the ball far enough'. At Woburn, she had no problem in keeping the ball in play, out of the trees, but always felt that she lacked distance. With a few simple adjustments to her grip and posture, Rina, rated one of the top 50 instructors, male or female, in the entire USA, had put that right. Now Joan says with undue modesty, 'It just proves that anyone can play golf!'

ANDY ROBINSON

According to Andy Robinson: 'The game is unique – anybody can play it and anybody, regardless of ability, can compete with the best players. Even disabled people, with all sorts of disability, even blind people, can play golf without any special privileges or concessions – the handicapping system takes care of that.'

Andy Robinson is six times World One-Armed Golf Champion. Andy was born in Southend-on-Sea in 1954 and, since his family included a grandmother who had been Essex Ladies Champion and keen parents who were 11 and 13 handicap standard, it was no surprise that Andy was on the golf course at the age of four, save that he was born lacking a right forearm below the elbow. But by the time he was 11, Andy was caddying regularly and beginning to put together scores.

At the age of 14, a chance meeting led to him joining the Society of One-Armed Golfers. He has not missed a World Championship since 1977 and won it in 1979, 1981, 1983–5 and 1989. Retirement from football (!) in 1981 because of knee-ligament injuries meant year-round golf and a steady improvement until he had achieved a handicap of 9.8 at his home club, Thorpe Hall, once the home club of Michael Bonallack, now secretary of the R & A and five times British Amateur Champion.

Our guinea pig parade as they line up for bunker instruction – from the left, Terry White, Harriet Rowe, Bryan Nickless, Danny Nickless, Andy Robinson, George Roberts, Ron Allfree and Joan White.

In 1992, the Society of One-Armed Golfers celebrated its 50th anniversary. The location was Ballater Golf Club in the Scottish Highlands, which was in its centenary year, and 61 members attended, from virtually all over the world.

Andy Robinson's ability as a disabled player brought him many invitations to play in charity golf 'Pro-Celeb-Am' events, at which Andy, to his embarrassment, was the celebrity. These events were run by SPARKS, the charity formed in 1960 by sporting personalities with the aim of raising funds for medical research. With an annual schedule of anywhere between 20 and 30 golf days the length and breadth of the country, the SPARKS people – in need of stronger administration – appointed Andy their full-time Director of Golf, and he is now dedicated to the organization for the rest of his life.

The Peter Alliss television series took Andy to Florida for the very first time, and a fascinating experience he found it to be. Since he joined SPARKS he had found less time to play, and 'my game needed shaking up – I had developed little faults', he said. 'I hit one shot and Bob Blegen, the coach, analysed my problem instantly. It was brilliant. Of course I have no right hand to complicate things, but it was reassuring to learn that teaching pros can analyse a handicapped swing so well. The imagery that pros can give you can be very helpful.' One of Andy's particular pleasures at the Walt Disney World Resort was in talking to and playing with Ron Allfree, the blind golfer and the other handicapped player in the group.

RON ALLFREE

Ron Allfree, pushing 60, was born in Kennington, South London, and is married to Maureen. They have three children. They now live in Sevenoaks, Kent. Ron first became interested in golf some 25 years ago, when a business chum invited him to play, and since then the game has been his passion.

He was employed by Beecham Toiletries for 25 years. About six years ago his sight began to fade and Sorby's Dystrophy was diagnosed. It is an affliction of the eyes about which not enough is yet known and Ron's vision deteriorated so much that he was obliged to accept early retirement. Now he can distinguish light and shade, but cannot see the golf ball when he is in the address position.

An article in the *Guide Dogs* magazine about the Society of Blind Golfers persuaded Ron to contact their chairman, Ron Tomlinson, and he has been very actively involved in the affairs of the society since then. When I, as patron, approached them to produce a blind golfer for the television series, Ron immediately declared his interest.

Ron is presently a member of Wrotham Heath Golf Club at Sevenoaks and is an active competitor in charity events for 'English Blind Golf', the charitable end of the society. For these, George Roberts is his guide and 'minder'. George, who plays his golf at the Horton Park Club in Epsom, is retired from business and has been a 'guide' for four years. 'Blind' golf is a team game and, without the service of guides, blind golfers obviously could not play.

On shots from tee to green, George will line up Ron so that his stance and posture are correct, and the clubhead is behind the ball. Ron then runs his right hand down the shaft to the clubhead to check the correct angle of the clubface. On putts, George will again line him up, but also tell him the distance, and how much to lay off for the slope. Ron will sometimes walk the yardage from ball to hole with George, to confirm things in his mind.

Ron's son Matthew, handicap six, who had been made redundant as a salesman with Benn the publishers, had decided to spend his redundancy cheque on a 90-day jaunt to America. He bought inclusive tickets from Amtrak and the Greyhound Bus Company, and covered the US very successfully. When he heard that his father was to be in Florida, he made a San Francisco–Orlando trip, one of the longest journeys possible in America, to be with him and join in the BBC fun.

THE 'PROS'

WALLY ARMSTRONG

Wally Armstrong has been teaching golf since 1968. A graduate of the University of Florida, where he earned both bachelor's and master's degrees in education, he was a member of the university golf team and 'All-American' in 1966. He became a PGA member in 1974 and has competed in over 300 Tour events. In addition, he has taken part in two Open Championships, two US Masters, seven US Opens and four US PGA Championships. He has a life membership of the PGA Tour.

Wally founded Gator Golf Enterprises in 1978 to concentrate on teaching and has become famous for teaching the feel and rhythms of the game to his students by using everyday objects such as brooms, mops, footballs and coathangers in a quest for visual imagery (see *Wally's Gadgets* on page 96). He has produced 13 instructional golf video tapes and has written extensively on golf instruction.

DONALD CRAWLEY

Donald Crawley was born and raised in Harrogate, Yorkshire, and played his junior golf at Knaresborough. He started a PGA apprenticeship with Murray Burgess at the nearby Pannal Golf Club. Donald met John Jacobs, another Yorkshireman, when in his teens and has pursued his teaching career under John's tutelage since 1975. He was British PGA Assistant of the Year in 1978, and played part-time on the PGA European Tour from 1974 to 1980, by which time he was head teaching professional for the John Jacobs Golf Centres in Britain.

In 1980 he went to the US to become a head instructor at the John Jacobs Practical Golf Schools USA and is now Director of Instruction for the John Jacobs operations in the US, Europe and Japan. As such, he conducts clinics for the 100 PGA professionals employed by John Jacobs and frequently lectures to PGA bodies worldwide. He now finds himself teaching at golf schools in Hong Kong and China.

BOB BLEGEN

Bob Blegen was born in Rockford, Illinois, but grew up in Wisconsin Dells, not far from Madison, Wisconsin. His father was superintendent of a small golf course, the Dell View Resort and Country Club, and

Bob grew up with the game, playing golf through high school and college. He earned All-American honours in 1984 at the University of Wisconsin, where he graduated with a BS in Physical Education.

His first contact with the John Jacobs organization came in January 1986. He was on vacation in Phoenix, Arizona, and met a college friend who was working at the school at Camelback Golf Club in Scottsdale. He was introduced to Shelby Futch, co-founder of the John Jacobs organization, and before he knew it he was enlisted. Now he is a head instructor at the Marriott Orlando World Centre in winter, and at Geneva Golf Club in Wisconsin in summer.

TODD HOWARD

Todd Howard was born and raised in the small town of Tolono, near Decatur, Illinois. By the age of 12, he was keenly interested in golf and was number one on his high school team for three successive years.

At 19 he moved to Arizona where, like Bob Blegen, he met Shelby Futch, co-owner and director of John Jacobs Golf Schools, and went to work for him in Scottsdale. He started a PGA apprenticeship under Craig Bunker, a Director of Instruction with John Jacobs Golf, as his assistant at the Davenport Country Club in Iowa. In 1985 he was the teaching pro at Skyland Golf Club, Crested Butte, Colorado. By 1988, Todd had become the youngest head instructor the John Jacobs organization had known.

Since then he has started many new golf schools, including Marriott's Orlando World Centre, Marriott's Seaview Resort, Marriott's Windwatch Resort, and the newest John Jacobs school, at Hana Country Club, New York.

RINA RITSON

Rina Ritson, from South Africa, is head professional at the Walt Disney World Resort's Lake Buena Vista course, and is one of the most highly regarded women teachers in America. Indeed in 1983 she was named LPGA National Teaching Professional of the Year and in 1991 was listed as one of the 50 best golf instructors in the US.

Her amateur career saw her win 15 championships from 1965 to 1970, when she became an assistant professional in South Africa. In 1979 she moved to Florida and has worked at Walt Disney World Resort since. She has written instructional articles for golf magazines, participated in many networked radio and TV programmes, made several video tapes and worked with several tournament players, among them Ireland's Ryder Cup man, David Feherty.

Rina has three grown sons, all in professional golf.

CARL RABITO

Carl Rabito has been a teaching professional at the Walt Disney World Resort since June 1984, much of that time as Assistant Director of Golf Operations. He has been involved in all aspects of golf – merchandizing, tournament organization, teaching juniors and conducting several workshops for other professionals on, for example, how to conduct junior programmes and the psychology of playing the game. He has a degree in business administration from the Louisiana State University.

NICK PRICE

Nick Price joined us to talk about difficult shots, awkward lies and stress in the game, and to play a few holes. He did not have to travel far – like many American tournament players, he lives in the Orlando area.

It would be pleasant to suppose we inspired him to win the US PGA Championship, which he did six months later, in the summer of 1992, for his first 'major' win. He had come close to winning our Open Championship, finishing second to Tom Watson at Royal Troon in 1982, and to Severiano Ballesteros at Royal Lytham and St Annes in 1988. Indeed for those of us with many years in the game, it was a delight to see Tom Kite in his forties win the US Open, and Nick, at 35, win the PGA.

Nick was born in Durban of British parents – his mother now lives in Norfolk – and grew up in Zimbabwe. For the past ten years he has played very successfully in America, winning the 1983 World Series of Golf, and in 1991 the Byron Nelson Classic and the Canadian Open, and in between times, the Swiss and Italian Opens and several tournaments in South Africa.

He is considered to be, technically, one of the most talented of contemporary players, with a beautifully controlled swing, quick and brisk. Nick is in the Watson mould – the address, the waggle, the swing, all brisk and businesslike. I have never seen him hit a shot off balance. He is always perfectly poised, as though posing for a photographer. He is also a thoroughly nice man.

Nick Price, who might just be the
nicest man who ever won a
championship, gets a few words of
wisdom. Nick joined us to talk about
difficult lies and awkward shots, and
delighted us all when he won the **US
PGA** Championship later in 1992.

19

JOINING THE CLUB

There is a conception in our country that every golf club is bulging with members and that getting into one, becoming a member of a golf club, is some kind of through-the-eye-of-a-needle operation. This is a misconception. For absolute beginners, for young people in general, it is not easy, but no one ever achieved anything by not trying, and it is seldom wise to make assumptions about this.

The first essential is to make contact with the club. If that contact can be made by a parent or a friend who is already a member, so much the better. If not, perhaps if the hopeful member has moved into a new area and knows no one who is a member of the club, he or she should simply telephone the club secretary for an appointment. The secretary will be happy to relate the membership procedures and costs. These

The most famous, and most photographed building in golf – the splendid, upright clubhouse of the Royal and Ancient Golf Club of St Andrews.

procedures will vary from club to club, but the basics remain the same.

The secretary may well arrange for the potential member to meet various members of the club committee. He may be invited to play the course with one or more committee members. Having found a proposer and seconder in this manner, his completed membership application form will be considered by a full club committee meeting. There may be an interview. In some clubs, a copy of the membership application form will be shown on the club notice board for a specific number of days, inviting comments from existing members.

At the end of that trail – short of any objections and assuming that there is a vacancy in the membership – our applicant will become a member and be expected to produce an entry fee. If the club has a waiting list, the applicant's name is added to it, and he waits upon events. Too often, the idea of a waiting list and idle talk of a two-year wait or a ten-year wait put people off. It is surprising how quickly these lists can melt away – with natural wastage (which in this case means death) and members moving away from the area, or veterans ending their golfing careers and so on. Of course, there are some clubs which one cannot simply apply to join, the best example being the Augusta National in the US. There, one doesn't ask, one waits to be invited.

THE HANDICAP

The handicap system is one of the glories of golf. It relates one golfer immediately to another. In horse-racing, a perfect race would be one in which all horses cross the winning line at the same moment. The system works in golf. The philosophy is to equalize the difference in talent between a scratch golfer and a virtual beginner. Just as it is in horse-racing, the handicap system in golf is less than perfect, but it does enable golfer A to play with golfer B in a system that brings them within reasonable reach of each other's scoring ability, and lets them have an enjoyable game.

A joint committee of the four golfing unions of Great Britain, at the request of the R&A in 1925, prepared the Standard Scratch Score and Handicapping Scheme which with some modification has applied throughout the country since it was introduced on 1 March 1926. The Standard Scratch Score of a golf course is fixed by its national golf union and is established for each club as the score which a scratch player is expected to return over its measured course. In establishing it, officials will take into account such factors as length, the general terrain, the hazards, the prevailing wind and the average weather conditions, the size of greens, the width of fairways, the nature of the rough, and so on. The allocation of handicaps is the responsibility of each club and can be allotted only to an amateur member of a club affiliated to the appropriate union. Although some clubs may apply the rules less rigidly than others, in general the handicap committee of the club will require the golfer to submit three cards, correctly approved, from rounds played in medal conditions over the measured course. In other words, three monthly medal scorecards of rounds played from the white tee markers. The committee will invariably discount any score on a single hole which is more than two over the par of the hole. If a player returns a score of nine on a par 5 hole, the committee will consider that score to be a seven, in calculating a handicap.

After these adjustments have been made, the committee will allocate the player a handicap equal to the number of strokes by which the best of these three rounds differs from the Standard Scratch Score. The maximum handicap is 28. There are various sophisticated mathematical procedures for altering handicaps up or down, depending on the member's form in future competitions, but all of that is the nub of getting a handicap in the first place.

But ah, you say, first you must become a member of a golf club. That's true, that's true – and this is Catch 22 with a vengeance. In so many cases it has been impossible to join a club without having a handicap *and* it has been impossible to get a handicap without being a member of a club! This is the situation which faces many golfers who play at municipal clubs or at pay-as-you-play courses, without a handicap, without membership of any golf club or society. This was the situation affecting young Paula Sainty when she was with us for the BBC filming in Florida.

With just this dilemma in mind, 'The Golf Club', Great Britain was formed by Bernard Pendrey in 1968, with the specific aim of tackling it. The GCGB created an 'International Handicap Register' as a means by which every golfer can obtain a properly monitored handicap. Anyone can join. There are family, junior and group memberships. All new members have to submit three correctly marked and properly attested scorecards for rounds played over measured courses. They are then given an initial handicap and are encouraged to return as many cards as possible, each time they play in fact. Changes to handicaps are notified to members on a monthly basis. All cards must be played under stroke-play rules. It was soon clear to the GCGB that members wanted more than simply a handicap service. Now the club has regional tournaments, a national championship, a directory of friendly golf clubs and an advisory service covering tuition, holiday golf and many other services. Its address: 3 Sage Yard, 302 Ewell Road, Surbiton, Surrey KT6 7AO (Telephone: 081 390 3113).

There is also help available for players caught in this Catch-22 situation from the National Association of Public Golf Courses. Secretary Alan Witte oversees all the clubs that play on public courses. It is usually easier and cheaper to join one of these clubs and they all allow their members to obtain an official handicap. This association is also developing quickly and has recently established national competitions for public course players of all standards, and 1992 saw the first such international tournament. Its address: 35 Sinclair Grove, Golders Green, London NW11 9JH (Telephone: 081 458 5433).

When you do eventually get a handicap, make good use of it. Use your strokes sensibly. The thing is not to be greedy. If the pin is cut tight behind a bunker, shoot for the middle of the green and content yourself with two careful putts. If your shot demands a carry over water, and only your best shot will make the carry, don't do it. Go round the water. We almost never play our very best shot to order.

Patience and common sense are needed in this game. Remember what the old caddie said: 'An eight is always one fewer than a nine.' And given a proper handicap, you can enjoy an absolute treasury of British golf courses, almost all of which will welcome you if you go through the proper procedures of calling or writing in advance. And I am not only talking about the great championship courses. I am thinking of Cruden Bay, Boat of Garten, Buchanan Castle in Scotland, King's Lynn, Littlestone, Blackmoor in Hampshire, Dooks in the West of Ireland, courses that are not too well known but are quite excellent. And some of the newer ones that I have been involved with personally I hope will give great pleasure to many people in time to come – courses such as Cambs Hall at Fareham, Castle Combe, Dummer, only 200 yards from the M3, junction 7, and Herons Reach, one mile from Blackpool Tower – a course I wager will host a major tournament within ten years.

Handicaps are a very important factor in the game. They are slide-rules which relate you instantly to your fellows, but they rise or fall solely by your own efforts, or lack of them. Cherish your handicap, polish it, bring it down!

ASPECTS OF THE SWING

KEEP YOUR BALANCE

Paula was the nearest we could get in our group to the classic 'absolute beginner'. She had been playing the game only a matter of months. The fact that Carl Rabito took her for her first individual lesson worked very well for her. Carl, our other Disney World Resort professional – Rina Ritson was the first – is something of an anatomist, and is very concerned with how the body works in terms of the physical movements required in the golf swing, how capable it is in 'helping' us to make a golf swing.

One of his first statements to Paula was that, 'Women are at a disadvantage when it comes to golf – in fact, to most sports. Most sports with a 'stick' – baseball, hockey, tennis – require a rotary action. The swing goes back and forward but above all, round. Hold your hands out, straight from the shoulders, palms up, hands touching. Let your elbows touch together. Good. Now did you know that most men can't do that? It's true. Now what happens is that when you swing a golf club back towards the top of the backstroke, you need to have the forearms supporting the club. With most women, the arms want to collapse, in the sense that the physical 'instinct' of their arms and hands is to collapse, the forearms and elbows touching, and the wrist falling over backwards so that the club flops down behind their backs. They'll say that they are not strong enough. That's nonsense, it is the simple business that their bodies don't work naturally that way, because of the structure of their shoulders and chest.

'In something of the same way, the hip "instincts" are different. When men walk, they walk tough, like Popeye, their hips rotating, but not sliding to the side, or outwards. When women walk, they "sashay" as we say in the States, their hips are inclined to move outwards and back in, side to side as it were. This makes for problems for them in the golf swing. Most women, on the takeaway and on the start of the backswing, are inclined to let their hips slide to the right. The most important thing in the golf swing, and certainly the most important thing in the set-up, is balance.'

Carl said to Paula, 'Do you feel you have balance?'

'Yes,' she said.

'Well, set up to the ball, as though you were taking a shot.'

She did and, with the index finger of each hand, Carl poked her lightly on the shoulders. Paula fell back!

'How to achieve balance?' Carl said. 'Stand tall. Imagine there is a shaft running down your spine. You are standing very straight. Your body is designed to bend from the hip socket – most people bend from

Paula concentrates hard on keeping that head still.

26

the waist, stomach, chest or wherever. But you must bend over from the hip sockets towards the ball so that the back line, the line of the spine, stays relatively straight. Maintain your face to the swing, head up. Your arms can now fall freely in front of you. Imagine if I had stood facing you, and pulled you slowly towards me by the collar, with you bending from the hips. With the knees slightly flexed, your weight would be more on the balls of your feet, and you would be balanced.'

Carl again pushed Paula's shoulders with his index fingers. This time nothing happened. She remained in balance.

'There are physical aspects to another golfing myth, the one about keeping your head down. Set up again, Paula, as though you were going to hit a shot. Keep the clubface behind the ball. Now close your eyes. Now let your head fall off your shoulders. Now lift your head up to the sky. Did the golf ball or the clubface or your hands move? No? So what did keeping your head down do for you? Not a lot!

'Paula, you hit some good shots, then hit what we call "fat" shots, which means you are changing height in the swing. You don't have to keep your head down, Paula, but you do have to keep it *still*. If you keep your head *down*, it restricts your left shoulder turning back on the backswing, your right shoulder turning through on the downswing. It prevents you from finishing your golf swing, so let your face relax! The golf swing is natural if you understand how the body moves. The golf swing is a pendulum. The ball is at the bottom of it. Underneath your face. If you are five feet tall, and stay five feet tall, you will hit the ball. That is a fact. The bottom of the pendulum is underneath your face so let the club swing, maintain the same height, and you will certainly hit the ball. The body, rotating, adds speed to the circle of the swing. That's what will make the ball go further.

'Finally, here's a drill for you. It's a good one for any golfer, not just starting golfers. Get set up to the ball. Draw your left foot back slightly, then lift your left heel off the ground. Swing back normally until you feel balanced as it were on your right hip. Start the club down, let your left heel come down and, as the clubhead strikes the ball away, stride through with your right foot, transferring all the weight to your left foot. And on practice swings, go right through to a high finish and hold it – your hands should be up by your face, or beyond, your weight should be on your left side, and your chest and stomach should be pointing down the target line, or even to the left of it. The whole thing should finish in perfect balance.

'And finally, realize that the golf swing happens very quickly. You have to learn it, understand it, understand why – and do it. But don't think about it too much.'

27

Rina Ritson shows
Joan how to get right
through the ball at
impact.

A LACK OF POWER?

Lots of people will say that the good lord did not design the female
form with the requirements of the golf swing in mind. I'm not so sure.
Bobby Jones used to say that the best golfer in the world was Joyce
Wethered, later Lady Heathcote-Amory. That was back in the twenties
and thirties and while times have changed, the fact is that the present
leading women players, on the US LPGA Tour, are hugely talented,
although they may not be comparable directly with Faldo, Ballesteros,
Strange and their like. Women golfers on the whole don't 'punch' their
weight as men do, or rather as men try to do, and we thought it would
be intriguing to put Rina Ritson, our renowned lady coach, in with Joan
White, our lady 'of mature years', and see what she made of her – or
of what Joan made of Rina, for that matter.

Joan had been suffering from a lack of power. She had no problem
with hitting those narrow, tree-lined fairways at Woburn, but she was

failing to get any acceptable length to her tee shots. Rina said, 'The set-up controls 70 per cent of what happens in the golf swing. By set-up we mean grip and stance and posture.' Joan's swing showed one of the classic faults of lady club golfers — she lifted the club straight up from rest on the backswing, letting her head sway away from the ball from an upright stance. Result? A cramped backswing, and virtually no energy being applied to the ball at impact. Rina said, 'The first thing we must do is adjust that grip. The left thumb heel pad controls the wrist, the wrist controls the clubface. That relationship is absolutely direct. So that left thumb heel pad must be firmly on the club throughout the action. Then your posture, Joan, is straight upright. That won't do. I want you to stand straight up, then bend from the pelvis, *not* from the waist, but from the pelvis, by sticking your butt out. Flex your knees slightly, and turn your toes out. Bow to the ball, then flex your knees. You are sitting easily on the front of a high stool now, eh? Now just swing straight back and through.'

CONTROL

There could be no greater contrast than that between Joan and Rina's next pupil, Danny Nickless, a 4-handicap teenager who was as lissom and fluent in his swing as you would expect. He had been fighting a lit-tle push/fade from the tee, and Rina quickly spotted a fault common to both golfers. She said, 'The right elbow position is a key in the golf swing. The position of the right elbow influences control of the units on the backswing. These units are hands, elbows, shoulders. If they oppose each other, work away from each other, or try to make any excessive rotation, then we are in trouble. The right elbow at address should incline towards the left elbow and the distance between them *maintained* throughout the swing. Elbows must be thought of as a unit.

'Control starts with the elbows. Danny gets into a good top of the swing position but here is a point I have to make with many tournament players — his right shoulder is inclined to start down. It should not. Let the hands and arms swing down to about hip high, then room has been made for the body to rotate, then the shoulder can come down, then the whole thing can turn towards the target. So for Joan it is butt out, toes out, flex knees, elbows together. For Danny, it is control with the elbows, get to the top, let arms and hands start it down, only then *rotate*!

'I don't use a method. I don't believe there is such a thing as a ''method'' in golf instruction. I teach people what's right for them. What's right for one may be wrong for another. I do have a pet peeve — left wrist control. If the left wrist is wrong, it makes it very difficult for

The joys of youth – Danny's full lissom swing caught in a splendid position at the top of the backswing.

the student to come into the ball correctly and generate some acceleration and clubhead speed. Here we had two very different pupils. Joan wants to hit the ball further. I definitely think we can get some power in there. There has been a restriction in her backswing which is not allowing things to happen. Danny by contrast is young, loose, an agile boy with everything going for him. I feel that his right shoulder is moving into the downswing too soon, and therefore he is getting to the ball with the clubface open.'

DISABLED PLAYERS
When Bob Blegen, the bright young instructor from the John Jacobs organization, learned that he would be teaching our golfers with disabil-

THE RULES OF GOLF

THE TEEING GROUND

The 'teeing ground' is the starting point for the hole to be played. It is a rectangular area two clublengths in depth, the front and sides of which are defined by the outside limits of two tee markers.

If your ball falls off the tee peg, or is knocked off as you address it, it may be re-teed without penalty. If a stroke is being made in these circumstances, that stroke will count, but there is no further penalty.

ities – Ron Allfree, the blind student, and Andy Robinson, our one-armed player – he reacted to the challenge very positively. It was to be something new in Bob's experience, and he prepared himself well. He spent half an hour on the practice ground blindfolded, and had Ron's guide, George Roberts, line him up exactly as he does for Ron, and Bob had some taste of hitting golf balls without seeing them. Then he spent half an hour swinging and hitting with one arm alone, the other tied down to his side, to learn how Andy had earlier hit a handicap mark of '9.8' as Andy insisted in calling it, 'not ten, please'.

Ron Allfree in fact is not what blind people call 'a total', meaning someone who has absolutely no vision at all. He can distinguish light and shade and can, for example, see George's outline. For example, on the teeing ground, he can see one of those square tee boxes perhaps two or three yards away. And his trick of checking his clubhead's relationship with the ball, when he has taken his stance, is intriguing – without moving his feet, and without releasing his left-hand grip, he bends over and slides his right hand down the shaft to check that the face of the club is square to his target line, behind the ball. With a white ball, he can see the ball shape then. Blind golfers, you might be surprised to know, play exactly the same game under exactly the same rules as do you and I. The only exceptions are that they are allowed to

Before teaching Andy Robinson and Ron Allfree, our students with disabilities, Bob Blegen spent half an hour swinging with one arm and swinging blindfold, to get some impression of how the game is for these men.

George Roberts, Ron Allfree's 'minder' checks that his man is properly set up for this fairway wood shot.

touch the ball when setting the clubface behind it, and they are allowed to touch the sand in a bunker. Ron plays to a handicap of 23, and for a couple of hours at Patshull Park near Wolverhampton, in the summer of 1992, he was World Champion! He led the championship until late on the last day, when a Canadian came in beating him by one stroke.

Frankly, Bob Blegen was astonished, having asked Ron to make a few swings, at what he saw.

He said to Ron, 'I'm going to move your grip slightly to the right, to get the clubface in a better position when it meets the ball. And on the downswing, I want you to "swish" that clubhead. That, combined with the grip change, will square the clubface at impact, so that the ball will fly in a straight line, instead of slightly to the left, where your shots are inclined to go. Don't hold it so tight! On the downswing, it is wrist, wrists, wrists, swing that clubhead.'

Ron was inclined to get his hands in front of the ball at impact, suggesting that he was not releasing his wrists so that the clubhead flashed through the ball. No doubt he was just a little nervous at the whole experience, but Bob assured him. 'Relaxing the hands will be at least fifty per cent of your problem. Please don't hold the club so tightly. You have a lot of good body action in your swing, Ron, but you have a

33

poor hand action. You need to relax your hands, have spaghetti hands. I think there are really only three things you should concentrate on – one is, beware of your grip, turn it slightly round to the right to square up the clubface at contact; two is to relax those hands; and three is to concentrate on making a swish under the ball during your swing.'

Bob's handling of that situation, the challenge of actually working with Ron, of understanding at least something of the world of golf that Ron knows, was quite exceptional.

He found that Andy Robinson, not surprisingly, had a very powerful left-hand grip. Born with a right arm shortened to just below the elbow, Andy has developed tremendous strength in his left arm. In fact he is a pretty solid, chunky character all round. After seeing him make a few swings, with the occasional hook, Bob Blegen told him, 'To be very basic about it, Andy, there are only two elements to a golf swing. The ball is on the ground. So arms and club have to swing up and down. And since the ball is at the side, there has to be an arc of swing that goes from side to side. As it does, the shoulders turn back, and on the forward swing, the hips turn through. We need both elements in the action. The fact that you are getting a little too much ground just before contact tells us that the shoulders are working too high, and too low, tilting in fact.'

Bob illustrated the point by holding out a club, hand at each end, shoulder high and parallel to the ground. 'We can fix that shoulder movement at address by raising the chin – an inch makes all the difference. If my chin, my posture, is down, my shoulders will tilt, high and low instead of round, resulting in crashing the clubhead into the ground behind the ball, pouring all its energy into the ground instead of squarely into the back of the ball. If I lift my chin up, and I exaggerate the point by using this club, I can make my shoulders work more horizontally. This motion drives the ball forward.

'Now the reason for your hook, Andy, is in the hip action. You now hit a good golf shot, but the ball is hooking slightly left, which tells us that in spite of you making a perfectly good backswing, the clubface is tending to close at impact, and so we have a hook. If you let your hips slide to the left instead of turning, they get in the way, they get stuck, blocked. But the clubhead keeps moving and, with the hips stuck, it will tend to close at impact, so the ball hooks to the left. On the downswing, the clubhead never stops, and it closes quite quickly. When that happens, it will hook the ball to the left quite dramatically. The whole ball of wax is: good posture, meaning a "taller chin"; right shoulder turns behind you, level; as the clubhead moves down to the ball, the left hip pocket is going to keep moving round to find the other

Andy Robinson, a strong young man with a very powerful leg action.

side of the golf swing. It is *not* going to slide. This is never a sliding or an "under" action. It is always a turning and a level action.

'So we want the left thumb almost straight down the centre of the shaft. (Andy had it powerfully round to his right.) I know, it will feel very weak and uncomfortable, but you must persist. And when your mind sees the ball hook to the left, it plugs into your muscles and the muscles react by driving more under the ball, and the result is you may now block it to the right. Too much ground at impact, too much turf just before contact, or at contact with the ball, tells you that there is too much of a rocking and blocking action with the shoulders working on the tilt, not on the level. So we want tall posture, right shoulder turning behind, left hip turning through, both level.'

35

THE SHANK

The shank is a dreadful affliction. It strikes the noblest of players. The shank describes what happens when a golf ball is struck not with the face of the club but with the hosel, the socket of the clubhead, that squiggly bit down where the shaft joins the head. The ball flies off furiously at right angles, completely out of control. This is also known as socketing or piping, and next to the air shot (a complete miss) the most embarrassing thing that can happen to a golfer. The late Henry Longhurst loved to relate how, when he was telling an acquaintance that he was suffering an attack of 'the shanks', this fellow said, 'Oh, I'm much worse, old boy – I'm a carrier!' You could picture him mooning around his club with a bell round his neck and a sign on his chest saying, 'Keep clear, keep clear – this man is a carrier of the dreaded shank.'

One person who did it often, if not regularly, was Dai Rees, in his time a Ryder Cup captain and a winning one at that. People maintained that this was because Dai had a loose grip, a two-handed baseball grip with the left hand very much underneath, showing no knuckles at all with the left hand. Socketing, I seem to remember, cost him an Open Championship at Troon back in the fifties, the one which Bobby Locke won. Dai was much in contention when on the 12th he drove down the fairway, then shanked into a bunker, took six or seven, and lost his chance for the Open. I've had only three that I can remember. Two of them were in bunkers, when I had the face laid back so much that I simply presented the hosel of the club at the ball. The other time was once on a practice ground, full of beans with about 20 people looking on, me poncing about as usual, taking deep breaths and looking terribly smart. I whipped a 9-iron out of the bag, one swish, one swing and bang! Away she went straight out of the pipe, leaving an embarrassed Alliss, pretending he had been distracted by something or other!

Some golfers have been known to shank putts and, although it is not something that can be cured in a couple of simple sentences, we can say that early symptoms are the pulled shot, when the ball flies straight left, with the face of the club pointing left, the divot pointing left. The shank has many causes. One is an insufficient shoulder turn, another is having rather static legs, yet another is if the head is lowered too much over the ball at address. Starting the downswing with a right shoulder movement will often do it. The ultimate reason for shanking is that the swing path has gone outside the line, outside the proper plane of the swing; the clubface is pulled across the ball and *shank*! The plane of the swing is the inclined line from the chin to the ball. Everything in the golf swing should take place 'inside' that plane. The shank is invariably worse with short iron shots, and pitching clubs. This is because they are precision shots where we are concentrating on pitching over a bunker or to a precise spot on the green, the type of shot in which we are focusing our minds on the destination of the ball perhaps more than on the swing. These are the shots in which increased tension, even fear, becomes a factor. One immediate treatment for this virus would be to raise the head and upper body at address, stand tall. Taking a more closed stance will also help counter the shank, but most of all what we need is confidence in concentrating on swinging the clubhead. It is good advice for every single shot in golf.

Dai Rees in his early days. An ebullient Welshman, victorious Ryder Cup captain, winner of tournaments galore and a competitor well into his sixties, Dai never let the occasional shank dent his love of the action.

37

The pitch to the sixth hole of the Magnolia Course at Disney World – nothing much to contend with – just a broad stretch of water, the huge Mickey Mouse bunker and a big sloping green.

THE PIN ACROSS THE WATER

The pitch shot across a hazard, with the flagstick cut rather close to the edge, is one of golf's frighteners. When the hazard is a bunker, that's bad enough, but when the hazard is a pond or stream, demanding a half or three-quarter shot with a pitching club, the situation can become ter-rifying for the club golfer. And if I say it shouldn't be, I'm liable to get a testy response. But this shot is like a bunker shot. It demands confi-dence and a sound technique. And, like every other shot in the golfing repertoire – practice.

During our filming in Florida, we found the perfect location to demonstrate all of this. On the sixth hole of the Magnolia Course at the Walt Disney World Resort, the ground slopes down to water in front of the green. Across the water, the ground rises to a green which is set quite a bit above the water level. On the upslope in front of the green is the famous 'Mickey Mouse bunker', a sand trap shaped in the outline of a big-ears Mickey Mouse. The pin was set quite a way behind the bunker. Such a shot requires a stroke which will get the ball up and over the water, long enough to carry *past* the water *and* the bunker, yet with enough control to land on the green and have it run just enough to the pin, and no further. In the event, we got Rob McNamara, the young American amateur and potential tournament professional, to demonstrate the shot from around 70 yards. He hit some lovely, posi-tive shots that ran close to the pin. The first thing to establish in your mind is that in this kind of situation the water and bunker are no more than distractions. As far as the technicalities of playing the shot are con-cerned, they do not exist. They do not hamper your swing in any way. The requirements are crispness of execution and firmness of decision-making.

Using a pitching club or a wedge, the weight should be on the left side, say at least 60 per cent with the ball slightly back in the stance to give a good position for driving the ball forward. The great thing is to keep the left wrist from collapsing on this stroke. If it does, you are in the water. You want a crisp downward swing, down to and through the ball. This is a simple hands and arms shot. Big backswings and excessive body action are *not* required. The feet should be only inches apart. Many club players have their feet so wide apart that they sway and get tangled up with ungainly movements. Instead of eliminating movement, they create movement, which is to be avoided. It is a simple hands and arms movement from a narrow stance. Excess movement only adds to the general confusion. Power is not needed. Crispness is all.

THE RULES OF GOLF

HAZARDS, WATER HAZARDS, LATERAL WATER HAZARDS

For beginners and inexperienced players, these terms and their differences and definitions are often confusing. But like most things in the golfing canon, they are less forbidding than they may seem.

A 'hazard' is any bunker or water hazard.

A bunker is a hazard consisting of a prepared piece of ground, often a hollow, from which turf or soil has been removed and replaced with sand.

A 'water hazard' is any sea, lake, pond, river, ditch, surface drainage ditch or open water course (whether or not containing water) and anything of a similar nature. All ground or water within the margin of a water hazard is part of the water hazard. The margin of a water hazard extends vertically upwards and downwards. Stakes and lines defining the margins of water hazards are in the hazards.

Water hazards (other than lateral water hazards) should be defined by yellow stakes or lines.

A 'lateral water hazard' is a water hazard or that part of a water hazard so situated that it is not possible or is deemed by the committee to be impracticable to drop a ball behind the water hazard in accord with rule 26-1b. (This rule relates to the action the player must take if his ball is lost in either of these hazards.) A lateral water hazard should be defined by red stakes or lines.

When a ball is lost in a water hazard, the golfer has two options, under penalty of one stroke in each case. He can drop a ball as nearly as possible at the spot from which the original ball was last played, or drop a ball behind the water hazard, keeping the point at which the original ball crossed the margin of the water hazard directly between the hole and the spot on which the ball is dropped. There is no limit as to how far behind the water hazard the ball may be dropped.

When a ball is lost in a lateral water hazard, the golfer has these two options, plus one other to consider. Another ball may be dropped not more than two club lengths of (i) the point at which the original ball crossed the margin of the water hazard or (ii) at a point on the opposite side of the hazard equidistant from the hole. The ball must be dropped and come to rest not nearer the hole where the original ball last crowned the margin of the hazard.

It is well worth having all this clearly established in your mind. It has been a source of lively discussion in many a golf match. So too has the business of cleaning the ball during all this palaver. It is permitted!

40

THE COX FORMULA

Bill Cox, a very successful teacher and a BBC commentator in the early days of televised golf, had a theory about lining up to the ball with the top edge of the blade rather than the bottom edge. Lined up with the bottom, he suggested, made it look open. Lined up with the top of the blade made it look square, or shut. Then on the backswing you had to break the wrists very early, swing slightly outside the line on the backswing, keep the club on that line, then drive down on it so that you came across the ball with a slightly shut face. You'd aim at the front left-hand corner of the green, and the ball would fade gently in towards the flag. Believe it or not, I took that idea with me in 1958 to the Italian Open, and won it; went on to the Spanish Open and won that; then went on to the Portuguese Open and won that, all in successive weeks, all with the Cox formula. Then, dammit, it was the end of the season, and by the time the Sunningdale Foursomes came round next spring, the magic had gone, never really to be recaptured.

THE BALL

There is something magical about being able to hit the ball a lot further than anyone else, and the man who does it better than anyone at the moment is John Daly, the young fellow who won the US PGA Championship in 1991. He really does smack that ball a long way. Most club golfers want to do likewise, but few of them seem to realize the advantages and disadvantages of using the right or wrong golf ball.

THE RULES OF GOLF

LIFTING AND DROPPING THE BALL

These procedures are probably the most misapplied in the game. When a ball has to be lifted under a rule which means it will be replaced, its position must be marked before it is lifted. If this is not done, there is a penalty of one stroke and the ball should be replaced.

If the ball or the marker are accidentally moved in the process of lifting or marking, there is no penalty. The ball or ball-marker should be replaced.

A ball being dropped under the rules should be dropped by the player standing erect, holding the ball at arm's length and shoulder height and dropping it. If it touches the player, his partner, either of their caddies or their equipment before or after it touches part of the course, it must be re-dropped, without penalty.

A dropped ball shall be re-dropped without penalty if it:
  i) rolls into a hazard
 ii) rolls out of a hazard
iii) rolls on to a putting green
 iv) rolls out of bounds
  v) rolls to a position where there is interference by the condition from which relief was taken
 vi) comes to rest more than two clublengths from where it first struck part of the course
vii) rolls and comes to rest nearer the hole than its original position.

Jose-Maria Olazabal, one of the world's top ten players in 1992, shows perfect dropping technique – arm stretched out horizontally, ball dropped vertically.

All ball manufacturers' products range in compression from 100, which is hard, to 90, which is of course a little softer. Players who don't hit the ball as far as they would like may be using a ball which is too hard. Various two-piece balls are made today. Compared to the traditional three-piece 'wound' ball, they will last longer, don't cut so easily, don't fade and draw so much. Some give a lower trajectory, which is good into wind, not so good downwind. So there is more than you may think to selecting the type of ball that will suit your game. Golf balls are expensive and a bargain is a bargain, but do take just a little bit of trouble to find the ball that actually suits your game.

THE RULES OF GOLF

THE PROVISIONAL BALL

The business of playing a provisional ball causes more uncertainty than almost anything else in the game. In plain terms, if you think your ball may be lost or out of bounds, to save time you can play a provisional ball from the spot where you played the original ball. You must tell your partner or your opponent that this is a provisional ball. If you don't, the original ball is considered lost, the provisional ball becomes the ball in play, under penalty of stroke and distance.

If you play a stroke with the provisional ball from the place where the original ball was lost, or from a point nearer the hole, the provisional ball automatically becomes the ball in play under penalty of stroke and distance.

If the original ball is not lost, the provisional ball is abandoned, and play continues with the original ball.

It is not enough to say to your partner, or opponent, 'Oh, I'll just knock another one up there.' You must declare the second ball you are about to play is a provisional ball.

A classic illustration of this arose at the Alfred Dunhill Cup event at St Andrews in 1992. In the match between Christy O'Connor Jr and Park Nam-Sin, the Korean golfer suspected that his drive at the 17th hole of the Old Course might be out of bounds, and he played a second tee shot. He failed to announce that this was a provisional ball, and when his error was pointed out to him failed to put it right as the rule required, before striking off from the next tee, and was accordingly disqualified. Many people at the time thought it a harsh judgement, but the rule is perfectly clear.

8 THE GRIP

We all chase perfection in golf and, in the chase, one of the things that is often ignored is the way we hold the club. The grip is fairly basic, basic to the whole operation of swinging a club and hitting a ball. The grip is the only contact we have with the golf club, in controlling the clubhead and how the clubface strikes, and therefore directs, the ball.

There are three recognized ways of holding a golf club. But before we consider them, we have to acknowledge the two absolute necessities in the golf grip. The hands must function as one unit. The palms of the hands must be facing each other on the club. And whichever grip we use, the hands will be touching. We are not swinging a pick here. The club lies across the bottom of the fingers of the left hand. They then close round it, with no gaps beween the fingers, and with the left thumb pointing down the shaft, not round it. The butt of the left hand

The 'Vardon' grip.

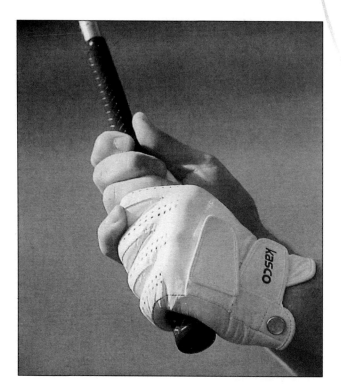

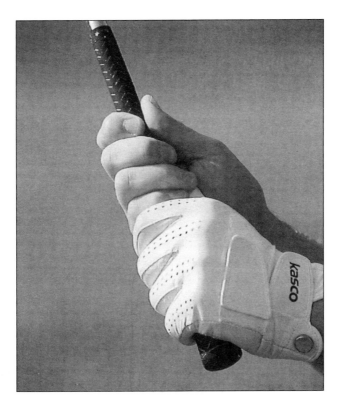

The 'Baseball' grip.

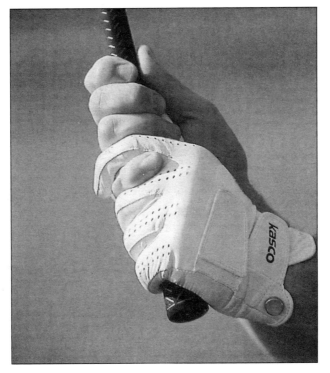

The 'Interlocking' grip.

Plaques at the South Herts Golf Club in North London where Harry Vardon was professional for many years, listing his honours and illustrating the Vardon grip.

wraps itself on top of the shaft, and the V formed by the thumb and index finger will point roughly towards the right shoulder. Then the right hand is wrapped around the club so that its little finger will rest on top of the index finger of the left, or between it and the adjoining finger. Again the V formed by the thumb and index finger of the right hand will point in the direction of the right shoulder. This is the Vardon grip, the one most golfers use.

The so-called 'baseball' grip has all the fingers on the club, but with the hands again working as a unit, palms facing. Art Wall, who won the US Masters, Bob Rosburg, who was a US PGA Champion, and Dai Rees, my Ryder Cup captain, all used the baseball grip.

The interlocking grip, the third of them, has the index finger of the left hand entwined with the little finger of the right hand and has been used by Jack Nicklaus, Sandy Lyle and Tony Jacklin.

These are the three possible methods of gripping the club. Whichever one you choose, it is important to get it right, and be comfortable with it. The other basic element in this is how tightly you hold the club. You do *not* hold it tightly, nor even firmly. Just enough to have it under control will do, and as I say, the most important thing with the grip is to *be comfortable*. You must never forget this.

Of course, there is another 'grip' in golf (and I don't mean a small bag). Just as a 'club' can be both a golf stick and an association of people who have joined together to play golf, so a grip can be not only how you hold the club, but the actual material on the handle of the club, or the handle itself. In times past it was invariably covered with leather. Your club professional may well have a training aid in the shape of a club with a grip moulded to take the player's hands and fingers, a 'grip for a grip'. Holding this club, waggling it, swinging it, will let you feel exactly how the hands should be set on a golf club.

Very often neglected is the condition of the grips on golf clubs. If you don't have a proper and confident grip on your clubs, it makes the game that much more difficult. Grips that are hard, shiny or have lost their tackiness simply need a wash — warm water and soap, properly dried, is as good as anything — two or three times a year. If they have lost a bit of tackiness, your club pro can help you. He will have a spray designed just for that, to put some tackiness back, particularly good for wet weather. But if you play a lot of golf, the best thing is to have the grips on your clubs replaced every year. That's a very good investment.

One obvious thing to remember, although we often see players who clearly have not, is to have a look at the condition of your glove. If it's full of holes, or you have to struggle and tug the straps to get it on or off, then buy a new one! Better to have no glove at all than an ancient and holey one.

THE SHORT GAME

Almost all UK clubs have very poor practice facilities. This is the historic process at work again. In the early days of golf, people were not much inclined for systematic practice, and so exclusive areas for practising were not considered necessary. Practice facilities on the Continent where new clubs are springing up are getting much better, but it's only when you come to the United States and some of its great resorts, like Disney World, that you can see how splendid and valuable practice grounds really can be. Having said that, it remains true that our club players simply do not practise enough. If they really wanted to improve their games, they would find a corner on their course, somewhere, to practise, without troubling anyone else. And since the short game is what it says it is – short, doesn't take up much room – and since a good 50 per cent of golf is short game and putting, we soon found a spot on the Magnolia Course to get to grips with it.

Donald Crawley, the exiled Yorkshireman who now works with the John Jacobs organization in America, had Terry White, handicap 14 from Woburn, and Rob McNamara, the young American hoping to do great things in time in professional tournament golf. 'Chipping and pitching' was the theme, and Donald placed Terry six feet or so from the edge of the green, Rob down a bank to the right of the green, unlike Terry quite a few feet beneath the putting surface. Thus he had simulated two common 'lies' in golf, which come when we are just short of the green with an approach shot, or find that our approach shot has run off and run down a bank. Two flags were set on the green, one 'near', only ten feet or so on to the putting surface, another 'far', maybe 30 feet on. As Donald said, 'A lack of distance from the tee can be compensated for by a good short game.' From these situations, the thing is to get up and down in two.

Terry was chipping balls with a 7-iron, but rather inconsistently. First he would hit 'fat', catching the ground behind the ball, then 'thin', catching the ball on the upswing, with the result that he had no control over the ball's trajectory or the distance it rolled. Donald explained, 'In all golf shots there are three constants – ball, club, swing. And there are three basics in chipping and pitching. The first and most important is *visualization*, imagining exactly how you want the ball to behave. The

second is in selecting the club that will make the ball behave in that way, and the third is in applying a swing to make it all happen. The difference between chipping and pitching is one of trajectory. In chipping we want to strike the ball on to the green and allow the ball to roll a controlled distance to the hole. In pitching, we want to land the ball further on to the green with a higher trajectory and a shorter, controlled roll to the hole. You must visualize exactly how you want the ball to behave. To have this settled in your mind, you may want to walk forward to the flag, check the distance, and see if there are any serious breaks, rises or falls on the green along the path you want the ball to run, which will affect your shot. The club you select will depend on what you have in the bag, of course. I assume you have a full set, but the reason I say that is that I don't want you to become limited to using just one club for chipping and running the ball. With Terry's 7-iron, I can de-loft it, down to a 6-iron or even a 5-iron, if I wanted to make the ball run further.

By de-lofting, I mean simply reducing the loft on the clubface by moving my hands slightly forward after I have taken a normal stance to the ball. In doing that, I will also move my feet slightly to the left. This obviously brings my right shoulder up slightly, which is exactly what we

Terry White gets in some chipping practice in the sun, under the eye of Donald Crawley from Yorkshire. Not all of Florida is flat.

51

THE RULES OF GOLF

LOOSE IMPEDIMENTS

Loose impediments are natural objects such as stones, leaves, twigs, branches and the like, dung, worms and insects and casts or heaps made by them, provided they are not fixed or growing, are not solidly embedded and do not adhere to the ball.

Sand and loose soil are loose impediments on the putting greens, but not elsewhere.

Snow and natural ice, other than frost, are either casual water or loose impediments at the option of the player. Manufactured ice is an obstruction.

Dew and frost are not loose impediments.

Except when both the loose impediment and the ball lie in or touch a hazard, any loose impediment may be removed without penalty. If the ball moves, there is no penalty.

Casual water is any temporary accumulation of water on the course which is visible before or after the player takes his stance, and is not in a water hazard.

Dew and frost are not casual water.

A hazard is any bunker or water hazard.

want, for it will give a steeper angle of attack on the ball. The clubface will be on its way down when it hits the golf ball, helping the ball to roll under better control. The ball should be in the centre of the stance. Terry, when using his pitching wedge, was addressing the ball too far forward in his stance, hitting up on the ball so that it became a scooter. The clubhead was coming in too shallow to the ball.

What is needed here is aiming the bottom edge of the club square to the target line; keep the ball in the centre of the stance; de-loft the club by moving the hands, then the feet slightly towards the target; let the right shoulder come up slightly, keep the weight on the left side. Then in going to a more distant pin, one on the far side of the green, say, when we will need much more roll on the ball, we don't change the technique, we simply change the club. Remember the three points – visualization, club selection, swing. The same swing with a less lofted club will send the ball further. We swing the arms and hands back –

not rigidly straight back, but with a little bit of an arc, from inside to straight on the throughswing.

Rob's problem was slightly different, and for different reasons. His lie, down a bank below green level, required a shot which had to be lobbed up to the putting surface with a much higher trajectory, and inevitably with a lot less run than Terry's pitch and run. Rob too was experiencing some inconsistency on the distance – making a reasonable contact with the ball, but hitting some shots long, some short. Again, it was a question of visualizing, then making a club selection, and finally

Donald Crawley sets young Rob McNamara right on the backswing, during pitching practice. Rob has had some success in amateur golf in America.

deciding on the length and pace of the swing. Where he was going wrong was with an undue amount of wrist cock when taking the club-head away from the ball. This causes an undue acceleration of the club-head, and gives an action that is a little independent of the body. On this shot, throwing the ball up to a green with a pitching wedge, the hands and arms and body should all move together. The top of the shaft should point to the belly-button throughout the action. The body should move back and through as the arms do. This will give a much softer shot, demanding a longer swing. Pitching to a more distant pin on the far side of the green will simply demand a longer swing. The swing stays the same, but the length and pace become important. We need to practise this — as in approach putting, touch and feel become important, and can only be learned by doing it, by practice! The old saying is (a) Understand it (b) Don't think about it (c) Just *do it*.

You might think of chipping as varying the club selection, and pitching as varying the swing length. With lots of green to work with, you don't have to pitch the ball a long way and have it land like a butterfly with sore feet. You can let it roll, as much as you decide. With Terry, our chipper, the thing was to have the ball in the centre of the stance, bottom edge of club square to target line, clubface de-lofted, feet more towards hole, right shoulder up slightly, naturally and an in to square swing path. With Rob, our pitcher, it was body movement and arm movement at the same speed and together; to make the ball fly lower, de-loft the club, to make it fly higher, loft the club. In all of these shots, you must practise so often that they become comfortable, with your technique fixed. Visualization, club selection, length and pace of swing!

THE SAND

Bunker shots strike fear into the average golfer. I wonder why. Well, I'm sure they all get fed up with me and my fellow professionals telling them just how easy it is to get out of the sand, but the fact is that it is easy – if you abide by certain basics. Most people play their golf at their home clubs, obviously, particularly in the UK, but increasingly they play in Europe on holiday and even travel to the US for golf so the first thing to consider is what kind of sand you have in the bunkers at your club.

If you play at the seaside and step into a bunker, odds are that you will sink down six inches in loose, soft sand, so you might need a sand iron with a wide flange. That will help your shot a great deal. If you play on the hard-baked courses of north London, where the sand gets compacted, you might need a thinner edge, more like a pitching wedge which will help a cut-up shot rather than a blast in which everything

The great Arnold Palmer can still splash his way out of hazards even in his silver years.

Wally Armstrong lays out his teaching aids for Paula, including the faceless and wedge.

comes out of the bunker in one glorious flowing movement. Then again, at courses on the Downs behind Worthing and Brighton, where the wind blows and the greenkeepers go potty trying to keep sand in the bunkers. . . !

In Florida the sand is very light and powdery. That can also make problems if there is heavy rain (yes, it does rain in Florida) when the sand goes gooey, like semolina pudding. But normally it is light and fluffy, like crushed marble. Of course, even the best of players have had problems with sand shots. Gary Player was probably the greatest bunker player of them all, the result of constant practice. But one remembers Fred Couples at the 11th hole at St Andrews in 1990 – first time he didn't get out, second time he didn't get out, third time he holed the shot! And poor Tommy Nakajima at St Andrews, on the 17th hole, when the Road Hole bunker cost him a nine. The great Arnold Palmer went one better at Muirfield in 1989, when a fairway bunker cost him a ten. Arnold could easily have played out of the bunker backwards – but that never was the Palmer style.

In our television series, Wally Armstrong had some interesting aids to help our pupils, Paula Sainty and young Matthew Allfree.

'They just have to remember a few basic principles of how to move the sand out, how to let the ball ride out *on* the sand. And the most

Gary Player, showing the style that has had him acclaimed as the finest bunker player of all – 'the more I practice the luckier I get'.

THE RULES OF GOLF

STONES IN BUNKERS

Stones in bunkers are 'loose impediments in a hazard' and therefore under the rules cannot be moved. In practice, many club committees make a local rule which permits moving such stones. The PGA European Tour, for instance, has decreed that for its purposes, stones in bunkers are 'movable obstructions' and can be lifted clear. It is always best to check on the local rules, printed on the scorecard.

The Armstrong 'two by four' with sand and ball on top. Demonstrating the point is Matthew Allfree.

important thing is to realize what gets the sand out of the bunker. It is not the face of the club, it's the flange, the flange at the bottom of the club that splashes the sand and the ball out on to the green.'

To illustrate this, Wally produced a sand wedge with the face completely missing, cut out. If you can imagine a club face with the centre section missing, the part where the grooves normally are, that's what he had. And promptly showed how it can work by splashing balls out of the bunker. 'Most people think it is the face of the club that scoops the ball out, but it isn't, it's the bottom of the club, the flange, and the ball rides up on a bed of sand. In bunkers, you want to think about moving sand, rather than hitting the ball. If you open the face slightly, that allows the flange to slide under the ball, and as it does, the sand will splash out.

'The sand will always fly in the direction the face of the club is pointed. So when you open the face, make sure it is pointed to the target, and move your feet and general stance around accordingly. Your body will then be slightly open towards the hole. With your weight favouring the left side, that will help the clubhead to go right through the shot.'

Wally's next gambit was to take a piece of two-by-four wood, painted red, and set it into the sand, lined towards the hole. He then puts a pile of sand on top of the wood, and invites his pupils to 'move that sand'. When they have done that properly, some red paint should

THE RULES OF GOLF

BALL PLUGGED IN A BUNKER

In a hazard, if a ball is covered by loose
impediments or sand, the player may
remove as much thereof as will enable
him to see the ball and identify it.

This is an argument for putting
identifying marks on an individual ball,
with a felt-tipped pen or whatever,
before teeing off.

Remember – you cannot ground your
club in a hazard!

show on the bottom of the flange on the clubhead. To remove the
paint, Wally simply gets them to take a few swings in the bunker,
splashing the clubhead through the flange. For his next trick, he has
them repeat the exercise, once more with a pile of sand on the two-by-
four, but this time with a ball on top of the sand – the instruction
remains the same, 'Move the sand!'

The next progression is that he will take an aerosol spray of paint,
make a circle, saucer-sized, on the sand, and have them splash that circle out of the bunker. Then, same again, with a ball in the middle of
the circle. 'These are great ways to practise sand shots,' he says.

To find out how hard to swing to get the ball up and out of the
bunker and also getting it to run as far as you want, to the flag, he says,
'I learned that by using a soccer ball. Standing side on, as you would
taking your stance for a golf shot, hold the ball in both hands, swing it
back and through, releasing it towards the target. Of course, I found I
had to open my stance somewhat, turn my body half towards the target
to get a proper release, but this practice teaches good arm movement,
and good judgement of distance.'

There is of course another basic sand shot. This is the one in which
we have to chop the ball out of the sand, or dig it out, when the sand
wedge becomes a digging tool and not a sliding or a gliding or a bounc-
ing tool. This is the one where the ball is plugged into the edge of a

bunker, when your approach shot, say, has just missed the green and buried itself – well, not quite buried itself – in the sand. The ball will probably be on an upslope towards the green, perhaps even rather close to the lip of the bunker. The first priority here is to get the ball out on to the green. If we can get it close to the hole, so much the better, but the main objective must be to get down in no more than three strokes from the bunker.

On this shot, you must have the clubface square. If you leave it open, the clubhead will splash when it should be digging. So square up the face of the club to the target line. If the ball is on a slight upslope, set your shoulders parallel to the slope. Then lean slightly to the left, which will set up a steeper angle of attack on the ball – not too much, or the club will simply bury the ball. You want a full backswing, ball in the centre of your stance, and punch down on the sand a couple of inches behind the ball. Make a strong, confident stroke, and you'll find that your wedge will dig that ball out perfectly well.

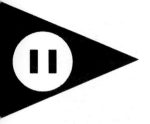

PUTTING

Doug Sanders and the
fateful miss – the 72nd
hole, the Open
Championship, the
Old Course,
St Andrews 1970.

This game of golf is difficult, in so many ways. We have 14 clubs, each there to do a specific job. And with each of these clubs, there are variations. We can play half shots, three-quarter shots, push shots, punch shots, high, low, pulled and faded and sliced. I cannot think of any other game that can compare in this respect. In tennis, there is serve, volley, forehand, backhand, overhead, lob, drop shot, then we are beginning to run out. And in golf there are other vagaries – the condition of the course, wind, rain, slow greens, fast greens, light sand or heavy sand in the bunkers. The permutations seem endless, they'd drive you crazy!

And so many of golf's problems arise when we get on the green. It doesn't do to ponder all those little putts that we miss. At the very top of the scale, at the highest level of the game, there have been disasters galore, and probably the worst of them, the one that will be written about as long as the game lasts, was that of Doug Sanders on the last green at St Andrews in the last round of the 1970 Open Championship. He had 'that to win the Open', a putt of three feet. It had been an extraordinary championship for Sanders. Forced to pre-qualify, he did that handsomely. Then on his very first hole, first hole first round, he dumped his second shot into the Swilcan Burn and scored six on the hole. When he got down in two from the Road Hole bunker on that last round, playing the most exquisite sand shot to make par on the hole, surely he had won the Open. But there he was, left with a three-foot putt to finally win. After he had lined up the putt, he suddenly leaned forward to pick up a piece of grit, on his line, when he might have done better to back completely away and start over again. He was looking at a downhill left to right putt, and when he finally did stroke the ball it slid across the hole, not even touching it, missing to the right. The next day, he lost the 18 holes play-off to Jack Nicklaus. Asked some years later if he often thought of it, Sanders said, 'Only every single day of my life.'

At the 1989 Masters, on the first hole of a play-off, Scott Hoch missed one, not much more than two feet, to halve the hole with Nick Faldo. At the very next hole, Augusta's 11th, Faldo holed from 25 feet for a birdie, and victory. On the last hole of the 1945 Masters, Ben

Hogan missed one from two feet to finish second. And John Cook, leading the 1992 Open, missed one from less than three feet on the 71st hole at Muirfield, and lost to Nick Faldo.

Of course, it depends where and when you miss the putt. And it depends who is watching. If it happens to be a television camera, then the entire world can see it. If a man loses a competition by one shot on the last, or second last, hole rather than the fifth or sixth, it is magnified out of all proportion. Craig Stadler missed a putt of no more than 18 inches on the last green at The Belfry in the 1985 Ryder Cup match. But, as Stadler said, 'It was on the second morning – there was still a lot of golf to be played.'

The bridge over the Swilcan Burn at St Andrews, the 18th fairway, the R&A clubhouse to the left.

When Bernhard Langer stepped up to his five-foot putt on the last green at Kiawah Island, in the last match of the last day of the Ryder Cup match in 1991, no matter what happened that putt was bound to be one of the most eventful in the history of the game. The entire Ryder Cup match hung upon this putt. If Langer holed it, he would win his match, the match overall would be tied, and the Europe team would retain the trophy. It was clearly downhill, breaking to the right. He hit it firmly at the hole, but missed on the right. It was a fitting ending, albeit cruel to Langer, to a fair and enjoyable contest.

The putting, the putting – 'It's aye the putting'. Dick Burton, the 1939 champion, putting all across the last green at St Andrews, is reported to have turned away when the ball was eight feet from the hole and tossed the putter to his caddie – he didn't even see the ball drop!

Of course, the tournament players always insist that the putter is the Achilles heel. I'm not so sure. They still miss fairways, still miss greens. The mathematics of the game haven't changed. It amuses me when they say that if you don't average 31 putts a round you can't make a living. Not true. If you hit all the greens and two-putt, you are round in 68 and four of these will win most tournaments. You can do a 68 with 36 putts and that's a fact of life. Many players are obsessed with the idea that they should always go for the pin. They are not that good. They are not using rifles. Go for the middle of the green, take two putts and occasionally on the law of averages hole one, and you'd be surprised what you can score.

On our Florida sojourn Todd Howard, the John Jacobs teacher, talked to our students and made sound sense.

'Most of the game of golf is played through the air, but with putting we have an entirely different element. Now we are concerned with rolling a ball along the ground. It's a game within a game. I always feel there are two basics to putting. One is technique, making sure we have the right grip, right stance, right posture, right aim, to hit the ball

Nick Faldo, for the past five years the best golfer in the world.

The relaxed Fred Couples, second to Faldo in the 1992 ratings.

The most charmismatic golfer of the age – Severiano Ballesteros.

Ian Woosnam, a Welsh bulldog.
Davis Love III, one of a new generation of top Americans.

Nick Price of
Zimbabwe, a 'major'
winner at last.

For Spain's Jose-
Maria Olazabal, a
first 'major' still to
come.

Paul Azinger, a US
Ryder Cup stalwart.

The man who 'should have' won a
Muirfield Open – John Cook.

Bernhard Langer and the agonies of
a Ryder Cup putt.

The stress of championship play – Greg Norman, just after impact.

Bernhard Langer at Kiawah Island, having missed the putt that would have tied the Ryder Cup match – 'the putt that no man should have been asked to hole!'

73

'Surely I can hole one
of these?' Nick Faldo
goes through his
putting paces.

solidly along the target line. The second is touch and feel.

'As far as technique is concerned, there are a variety of strokes and grips. What is essential to know is that the grip controls the face of the club and the face of the club must be square to the target line at impact. Any kind of grip on the club will do, the Vardon grip, baseball grip, interlocking grip, separated hands grip, even the Bernhard Langer, in which the right hand clutches both the handle of the club and the left forearm (!), but no matter which grip is used, the palms of the hands must be facing each other, or opposed, and the thumbs should be down the centre of the shaft. The eyes will be directly over the ball when the stance is taken and the ball position should be in the middle of the stance, or slightly forward of that.

When you get to the green, it is important that the first putt is close enough to make sure that this will not be a three-putt green. That may be obvious. It is certainly critical. Three-putt greens destroy a score. So it is very important to look from behind the ball to the hole to see if the line runs straight, or right to left, left to right. Also, look at the putt from the side. You can judge then how far the putt must travel and note the rise and fall of the green between ball and hole. Actual distance is not so important. What you want is a mental picture, so that you can develop ''touch and feel''. All the top players take a couple of practice swings. They are getting the feel of the stroke. We need to rehearse the length and pace of the putt, then commit to that stroke.

'There should be a minimum of wrist action. Movement of the wrist means movement of the club. To putt successfully, we need to have the face of the putter going through the back of the ball squarely at impact. Posture should be upright, shoulders square, parallel to the target line. A posture too much over the ball, crouched, means that the putter head will swing down too steeply into the ball. It should move parallel to the ground as it strikes the ball.'

Howard's way is the right way. But there are one or two points that I should make. Bobby Jones said the closer we get to the hole, the more fear begins to dominate the mind, and perhaps the most positive asset we can have on the putting green is confidence. We would all do well to imitate Nick Faldo. Like all of us, he has had his problems with putting, but in the second half of 1992, perhaps the greatest sustained spell of form in his career, he looked as though he would hole every single putt he took. Confidence with the short putts, the three, four, five and six footers, is the thing.

The biggest single problem with putting, for all golfers, is movement, movement of the head, and general body movement. Putting

THE RULES OF GOLF

THE PUTTING GREEN

Putting-green dos and don'ts are mainly don'ts.

The line of putt must not be touched except:

the player may move sand and loose soil and other loose impediments by picking them up or brushing them aside with his hand;

in lifting the ball, or in measuring the putt;

in pressing in a ball-marker;

in repairing old hole plugs or ball marks on the green;

in removing movable obstructions;

in addressing the ball, he may place the club in front of the ball but without pressing it down.

A ball on the green may be lifted and cleaned.

The player may not test the surface of the green by rolling a ball or roughening or scraping up the surface.

The player shall not make a stroke from a stance astride or with either foot touching the line of putt or an extension to that line behind the ball.

When a ball overhangs the lip of the hole, the player is allowed time to reach the hole without unreasonable delay, plus an additional ten seconds to determine whether the ball is at rest. If the ball by then has not fallen into the hole, it is deemed to be at rest and must be played.

should be hands and arms only. Any other movement breeds inconsistency. You should not break your wrists. Lock them. But if you have played all your life with a wristy putting action, it will be too late for me to think of changing you. The best way to avoid any unwanted body movement is to focus on the ball and keep your focus on that same spot long after the ball has left on its way to the hole. Lack of patience, anxiety to see the ball roll even before it has been struck, perhaps causes more missed putts than any other single thing. Lack of acceleration is critical. A long backswing, with the putter head decelerating as it reaches the ball, means that the contact will be insipid, the ball will not reach the hole and it will probably be squirted off line. To combat this, the through stroke should go well past the ball on a straight line. The putter

head should keep moving after contact, with the through stroke twice as long as the back stroke. Be positive and you will improve your putting.

If the putter blade is not square to the target at impact, the ball will be either pulled left or pushed to the right. Lining up with the blade square to the line is the single most important thing you can do in preparing to putt. Make sure you get that right. In making the stroke, you should have the feeling that you are taking the putter head straight back from the ball, then straight through the ball along the line. The putter head will come slightly inside the line on the backswing, but you should not do that deliberately. Take it back, swing it straight through. If you watch the finest players on television, you will see that in almost every case the wrists do not break and the player is very still during the entire stroke. The head does not move. Movement of any kind is held to a minimum. Grip, stance and ball position are highly individual. However these are used, they must allow the golfer to swing that putter head square along the correct line, accelerating on contact with the ball.

Todd Howard unravels the mysteries of putting for our squad, and our cameras, at Disney World.

77

The golfer can prepare himself for the putting game as he approaches the green. He can establish the 'tilt' of the green, how it lies, sloping to the left or right, back to front, or whatever. If he has had to chip a ball on to the putting surface, the roll of the ball across the green will give him a good clue to its contours. Since every putt requires distance and direction, the contours of the green determine the line the putt must take. One important factor on direction in places like Florida, where the climate affects the grain of the grass, is to establish how the grain will affect the path of the ball. Experience makes knowledge in this respect. The distance factor comes with experience, knowing just what weight to put on the swing to get the required distance.

Persuading yourself that every putt is straight will certainly help your confidence. Once you have decided the line the putt should take, you hit the ball *straight* along that line, and allow the contours to take the ball to the hole. And one of the very best ways to help yourself have the confidence to do this is to pick a spot 12 inches in front of the ball, and putt over this mark. That will work wonders for you!

ADVICE FROM PRICE

One of the most intriguing aspects of the game of golf is that Nick Faldo and Severiano Ballesteros and all the international champions at the height of the professional game operate by and large under the same Rules of Golf as does the modest golf club member playing in his club competition. Local conditions may occasionally require local rules which are additions to rather than variations of the Rules of Golf, but for all practical and general purposes, in golf we are all, as the Scots say, 'Jock Tamson's bairns'. (And don't ask me the origins of that one!)

When Nick Price joined us briefly during the filming in Florida, the girls, Harriet and Paula, were terribly nervous about playing with such

---

THE RULES OF GOLF

GROUND UNDER REPAIR

Ground under repair is any portion of the course so marked by the committee. It includes material piled for removal, and any hole made by a greenkeeper, even if not so marked. Stakes and lines defining ground under repair are included in such ground. The player may lift and drop the ball without penalty at a point on the course nearest to where the ball lay, provided it is not nearer the hole, not interfered with by the ground under repair and not in a hazard or on a putting green.

Nick Price has a champion's advice for Harriet.

Ian Baker-Finch, the enchanted champion, Royal Birkdale Open Championship, 1991.

a great player. Nick quickly put them at their ease by saying, 'We all get psyched up. What most people overlook is that everyone can get nervous when faced with certain situations, and it is the same with golfers. The better you play the game, the less nervous you will be about it. In tournament golf, they talk about us getting into "a zone", being able to concentrate so much on the golf that you don't think of anything else, you don't think about the crowds, the weather, the environment, simply the golf shot itself, and playing the shot.' One outstanding example of that would be Ian Baker-Finch in the last round of the Open Championship of 1991 at Birkdale. He scored the first nine holes in 29 and played like a man entranced – which he was. Nick Faldo has been able to do the same thing and, as Nick Price said, 'It is a wonderful feeling when you do it.'

Nick was quick to point out that the Rules of Golf should not be considered a catalogue of penalties, but rather a code to protect the golfer from the things that can happen in play, and a code that should be used to the golfer's advantage. The 18th hole on the Palm course at the Walt Disney World Resort is 454 yards, running between trees with fairly hefty undergrowth on either side. As we played the hole, Nick used it to illustrate some difficult lies. For example a ball hit just

THE RULES OF GOLF

OUT OF BOUNDS

Out of bounds is ground on which play is prohibited. When it is defined by stakes, or a fence, the out of bounds line is determined by the nearest inside points of the stakes or fence posts, excluding angled supports.

When defined by a line on the ground, the line itself is out of bounds. The line extends vertically upwards and downwards.

The entire ball must be out of bounds. A player may stand out of bounds to play a ball which is in bounds.

The ball should be re-played from its original position under penalty of one stroke.

off the fairway could easily finish among some roots.

'The first thing to happen with any difficult lie,' Nick said, 'is to establish clearly in your mind exactly what the situation is that you are facing. Only then, decide how to deal with it. A ball lying in these roots is a classic case of an unplayable lie. In addition to the roots, the ball is lying under some branches, and we could spend all day trying to hack it out of there, and probably break a wrist into the bargain. The rules allow us some relief. We have three options. One is that we can drop a ball within two clublengths of the unplayable position, not nearer the hole. That would leave us still among the roots, so that one is not practicable. The second option is that we can mark the spot where the ball is and go as far back as we please, keeping the mark in line with the hole. In this case, that would put us further into the woods, so that's no good. In this case we have to take the third option, which is to go back to the tee, or wherever we played the ball originally, and simply play another ball. In each case, there is a one-stroke penalty. When

dropping a ball and taking relief, remember that a ball might roll into more trouble, so don't be smart. Accept your penalty, cut your losses, and get on with it.

'Another common situation is to find your ball under a bush or a tree in a position which compromises your backswing. You could try to play it out left-handed of course, but I wouldn't recommend that. What you can do is stand on the "other side" of the ball, turn your back on the hole, reverse the clubhead and just chop it one-handed back out on to the fairway. With a little practice you'd be surprised how easily you can do that. You'll make it difficult for yourself if you try to hit it too hard, get too greedy in other words. All you really want to do is get it

The old boy, game as ever. Nick Price, Harriet and Paula look on in wonder.

83

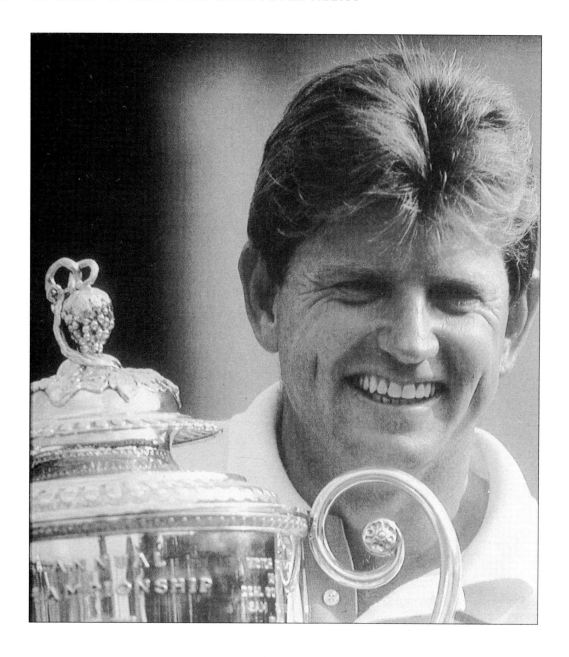

Nick, the smile and the spoils of
victory – the huge **US PGA**
Championship trophy which he
won in 1992.

THE RULES OF GOLF

UNPLAYABLE BALL

The player may declare his ball unplayable at any place on the course except when the ball lies in or touches a water hazard. The player is the sole judge as to whether his ball is unplayable. If the player deems his ball to be unplayable, under penalty of one stroke, he may:

a) play a ball as nearly as possible at the spot from which the original ball was played;

b) drop a ball within two clublengths of the spot where the ball lay but not nearer the hole, or

c) drop a ball behind the point where the ball lay, keeping that point directly between the hole and the spot on which the ball is dropped, with no limit to how far behind that point the ball may be dropped.

If the unplayable ball is in a bunker, the player may proceed as above except that under clauses (b) or (c) the ball must be dropped in the bunker.

back out into the fairway. A situation that calls for another common-sense approach is when you find your ball on the bank of a bunker, well below feet level. Basically, you want to get the ball back on the fairway. I'd take a lofted club, a 9-iron say, widen my stance, get right down to it, choke down on the shaft and just chip it back out, down the fairway. That's all you need – don't be too smart or too greedy.

'What many people don't understand is that when you take relief, you must take it at the nearest point of relief that the rules require. For instance, you might find your ball on a path, touching the grass verge.

This is more likely to happen in the United States, where so many courses have paths built specially for golf carts. The nearest point of relief in that case would be only a few inches from the ball, on the grass verge. So mark that spot with a tee peg, then drop the ball within one clublength of that point, not nearer the hole. It would not be permissible to take the ball to the other side of the path, for instance – that would not be the nearest point. And if you followed the above procedure, then found that the new lie of the ball was under some branches for example which hindered your stance or swing, taking relief from that would be taking relief from an entirely different situation. People don't always understand that the relief was from the path, as it would be from an immovable obstruction. There is no penalty. When relief is given without penalty, the ball is dropped one clublength from the spot. When the relief is being penalized, as in an unplayable lie, the ball can be dropped two clublengths from the spot. But in every case, with puddles, ground under repair, whatever, it must be taken at the *nearest* point.'

Golfers have handicaps, set by the committee. That means on certain holes they have complimentary strokes. They should use them sensibly. The majority of players simply dissipate them. As Nick said, 'How many people do you know who say, "I played so well, and if I hadn't made a nine on that hole . . ."' In his case, of course, as with all the top players, it is usually 'If I hadn't missed that three-footer.'

Price incidentally, while acknowledging that the world of golf has grown enormously, does not think it is becoming too big. He told me, 'There are so many good golfers in the professional game today, and so many youngsters coming through, that there must be a place for them to play. If the game is to get better, it must have some depth to it.

'The Ben Hogan Tour in the United States is secondary to the big PGA Tour, but is a proving ground for the younger fellows. Lots of very fine players have emerged over the past few years and are now doing really well on the main tour. I understand that the European Tour also now has a supporting tour, which is growing. Without these structures, these fellows would have a really hard time breaking into tournament golf. So the more tournaments we can get the better. Certainly the game has improved tremendously in so many areas. Apart from clubs and balls, the preparation of golf courses has shown a dramatic improvement in the past 25 years. The technology in maintenance, course equipment, and the work the agronomists have done with hybrid grasses and their treatment has meant things have become better and better. It's never ending. I don't know what we will be playing on in the year 2000 – but I'm looking forward to it!'

SEVE, NICK AND BEN

Severiano Ballesteros, I suppose, would have to be the seminal figure in championship golf in the last quarter of the 20th century, not so much for the events that he has won, but for the manner in which he played the game, and for inspiring European players to end the dominance of America. His play was that of a natural athlete, a golfing original, completely divorced from the manufactured brilliance of Ben Hogan, subsequently personified in Nick Faldo. It would be no exaggeration to say that the stature of Ballesteros in the game was greatly responsible for the fact that in the hallowed matches against the Americans – the Walker Cup, the Ryder Cup, the Curtis Cup and,

Nick Faldo with an old friend, the Open Championship claret jug won three times in five years – Muirfield 1987, St Andrews 1990, Muirfield 1992.

more recently, the Solheim Cup involving women professionals – the Great Britain and Ireland, or the Europe, teams won. In the past, pre-Ballesteros, victories in these events were scarcely imaginable.

I never did think that Severiano's relatively bad form in the middle of 1992, indeed in all the major championships of that year, would last long but having said that, some of the great ones have 'gone' quite quickly. Tony Jacklin came back to earth fairly quickly after his golden spell at the turn of the seventies. He played on for five years, ten years, but just seemed to have slipped a gear – there, present, but not really doing anything comparable. But his was not quite as dramatic a collapse as those suffered by Sandy Lyle and Johnny Miller. Tom Watson stopped winning, started missing a few putts. That's when self-doubt creeps in, you wonder if you'll ever get that little bit of magic back. But all the great ones come to the end of a career at some point.

Some go on and on. Many people think it sad to see Arnold Palmer battling away in the senior ranks, but he loves the game so much that who is to say he shouldn't? He has always said that the moment *he* feels embarrassed, he'll pack it in. This kind of decision must always be left to the player. The observer may say critically, 'What a pity, shouldn't he have retired sooner?' In cricket you get a Ted Dexter who perhaps retired much too soon. A fellow called Peter Alliss certainly retired too soon, dammit – only 39, and full of fight!

After Nick Faldo won the 1992 Open Championship, the writers started to compare him with Ben Hogan. This I thought was unfair. Hogan is Hogan, Faldo is Faldo. As the man said, 'Diamonds are diamonds, rubies are rubies, pearls are pearls.' In so many ways Hogan has been a better performer than Faldo. And they could scarcely be more contrasting in almost every regard. Hogan had to use inferior equipment, and did more with it. The Second World War took a couple of years out of his career. A fearful automobile accident took another year out of his life. His early days were a constant struggle. He was a product of the caddie shed. He did not have the luxury of an amateur career. His father committed suicide when he was nine years old. Hogan was at best 5ft 10in tall. Faldo is 6ft 3in, the only son of middle-class parents. He was able to indulge in an amateur career which brought him the English Amateur Championship before he turned professional. So they have been different in stature, physique and early privilege. Ben Hogan was a late developer. But what they have in common is overpowering – their dedication to the search for perfection.

I found Hogan a very interesting man. In the couple of brief conversations I had with him, when he captained the US Ryder Cup team at The Champions course in Houston in 1967, I felt he had a great pres-

Severiano Ballesteros
in sunshine mood –
that one must have
dropped.

ence. I suspect he thought he was under-educated, and had something of an inferiority complex about his early life, and so it was not arrogance that made him reluctant to appear before the public, or make speeches. It was perhaps shyness – echoes of Faldo?

I've got a letter from Hogan tucked away in my files. We asked him to appear on camera with me and he wrote back a charming, 10-page letter saying he hoped I would understand that 'he felt he wasn't any good at that sort of thing, and would I please excuse him for not taking part'. It showed a side of his nature that not many people are aware of. Lots of them think him rude, distant and offhand and I daresay he has been those things on occasions. So has Faldo. Faldo's golf over the past five or six years has been remarkable by any standard. He has worked hard and diligently, he does an awful lot of charitable work that doesn't get much recognition. He doesn't seek it, which is even better. I have been intrigued to see that both Ballesteros and Faldo are becoming more and more active in the business of golf course design. Ben Hogan never did aspire to that business. What a shame – it would have been fascinating to see a Hogan course, would it not?

**Ben Hogan,
Carnoustie 1953.
After a life of
struggle, in one single
year he won all the
game's most
cherished
championships, the
US Masters, the US
Open, the Open
Championship.**

91

14 THE ALLISS INTERVIEWS

Your man, Rina Ritson and Joan White watch young Danny Nickless shape up to an approach putt.

RINA RITSON

Q *'Rina, you have been head pro here for 14 years – seen many changes?'*

A 'Tremendous changes, Peter, in the expansion of women's golf.'

Q *'Interesting thing is that I doubt whether there is more than a handful of women in golf in Britain who are head professionals at golf clubs, and yet here, what have you got, twenty or thirty thousand teaching professionals. What percentage of these might be women – quite a large percentage?'*

A 'I would say a minimum of 15 per cent.'

Q *'Why do you think that is? Whose idea was it to have women teach women?'*

A 'It started in the pro shops, where the professionals found the girls did a better job, were more meticulous. They helped with the purchasing, were really good with the guests, members and customers. The business of becoming teachers evolved from there.'

Q *'You have played and worked at the highest level, in running this big facility at Lake Buena Vista — do you think more men would learn more about their game from watching good women players than from watching macho men?'*

A 'The average guy, from 12 to 25 handicap, could learn more from the girls. The girls are not powerhouse swingers, more the finesse type of swingers and golfers.'

Q *'Any resentment from males?'*

A 'I wouldn't say resentment. There was a segregation-type thing, along the lines of this was a man's world and suddenly here were women appearing in that world. I can remember in my early teaching days, the students were men, and little kids. Now it is women who are booking the lessons — in many cases they are playing and their husbands aren't, so now they bring the husbands and introduce them to the game!'

RON ALLFREE

'I haven't had any problems in terms of being blind and a golf club member. I had been a member of Wrotham for a number of years. The club is quite happy for me to be there as long as someone is prepared to play with me, but of course I have heard that there can be a problem with disabled people joining clubs. In particular, there was a man down in the south east [of England] who had been a member of a club for some 20 years and when his sight started to go, he was asked to leave. He was very upset about it.'

Q *'The thinking being what?'*

A 'The thinking being that he would be a danger to the rest of the people on the course, that he would not be able to see where other people were. I couldn't really see the point. If his sight was that bad, he couldn't have played on his own, and the people with him, minding him, would have said, ''Hold on, you can't play yet.'' Rather petty, showing no understanding of people with a disability.'

Q *'For people who have had sight, which gradually dwindles, there must have come a time when they need help — you yourself for example becoming virtually blind after a period of nine or ten years. Do you find yourself helping people?'*

A 'Blind people don't want to be considered disabled people. We want to be considered as people who just happen to have a disability.

They want to continue to play their sport when they can. I help others in that way as much as I can.'

Q *'Does your wife play golf?'*
A 'No, but she's become used to it all, because I've played for 25 years, and my son plays to quite a good standard. She enjoys walking around the course – she brings the dog and walks with me. But after a few odd experiences in guiding for me, she doesn't do that any more.'

Q *'She guided for you?'*
A 'Yes. We played once at Leeds Castle. We get up to the first green, a long par-4, at that time skirting the moat, although they have changed it now. I had two fair shots and was reasonably near the green. I said to Maureen, "How far is it to the flag?" She said, "Oh, I've no idea of distances." I said, "Well, you must have some idea." She said, "It's about as far as from our back door to the greenhouse."

'I knew the distance so that was fine – everyone else thought it

Ron Allfree prepares
to putt on the par-5
18th hole at the
Osprey Ridge Course.
He holed it for a score
of 5.

was hilarious. But I just thought that provided I didn't hit the thing further than the length of our garden, I'd be all right.

'I'm the only blind person at our club — there are probably others, but they won't admit it!'

FOOTNOTE

Ron and Andy Robinson played the 18th hole of the Osprey Ridge Course at the Walt Disney Resort, a par-4 of not quite 400 yards. Ron, being set up as usual by his minder, George, hit two nice wood shots down the fairway, then a 7-wood to the back right corner of the green. Andy hit a drive and a 6-iron about 20 feet from the hole, which has a rash of bunkers in front of the green, and a lake all along the right side. Andy two-putted for his par. Ron, with George's help, hit his first putt, from 26 yards in George's judgement, four feet past the hole — and holed the return, score five.

WALLY'S GADGETS

Wally Armstrong is a Florida man and a golf teacher who takes an impish, but innovative, attitude to the business of teaching the game. And as much as anyone can, he puts fun into the game by showing how everyday artefacts can be used to give a permanent mental picture of the swing and aspects of the swing. He is quite convinced that these 'pictures' and the feeling of the physical movements which they demand are worth thousands of words, and a 'hands on' approach to the student. Hear, hear, I say.

For example, he uses a coathanger, which grew out of the domestic article that dry-cleaners use. By holding the straight leg of the hanger and the golf club at the same time, it can help the golfer take up a correct grip. The hook part of the hanger would be between his arms, pointing up towards his face. At that time, no part of the hanger would be touching any part of the player's body.

On the backswing and at the first cocking of the wrists, the hanger gives an instant feedback. A proper wrist cock and arm action on the backswing is needed to support the club on its way back, but if the hanger touches a forearm, the wrist cock is wrong. This fact could almost revolutionize women's golf – they have a tendency to lift the club, let their arms and elbows work closer together and, towards the top of the backswing, let the club fall slightly, or 'lay off' as we say. Do it right, ladies, and the arms of the coathanger will not touch the arms of the golfer. That same fact applies to the rest of the swing, down-swing and follow-through to completion. The hanger can be used effectively on its own, at home for that matter, to check correct wrist cock and all the rest of it. Brilliant, simple, cheap – Wally is a wonder, a thinking wonder.

Armstrong has also devised what he calls a 'teaching station', which is essentially three rulers joined, or rather three rulers each about a foot long and hinged together. For long putting practice, it is laid in a shallow 'U' pattern behind the hole, providing a cave into which to putt. Laid on the ground on the tee, it becomes a teaching station which helps set up the stance, ball position and positions of the feet, and can set the clubface at right angles to the target line. Used this way, it is laid as, this time, a right-angled 'U', with the centre ruler at right

angles to the target line, and the other two legs parallel to each other and to the target line, with an 'open' side towards the hole. The player can then set the ball just beyond the central ruler, in line with it, adjust his stance and body 'set' accordingly, and set the clubface beyond the centre ruler, behind the ball and square to his target line. Again simple, cheap, can be used indoors, and much easier to see and use than it is to describe!

Wally has used ice-hockey sticks, mops and brooms in seeking to reveal some of the mysteries of the golf swing.

One of his more intriguing creations is the 'Tempo Ball', of the order of some medieval mace – a golf shaft cut off just below the grip, a piece of cord attached with a soft rubber ball fixed to the other end of the cord and the whole thing adjusted to the length of a 7-iron. The thinking behind it is that the greatest single quality people need in golf, particularly when they are starting, is a sense of tempo. By swinging the Tempo Ball at a correct and regular tempo, simulating a golf swing, the

Wally Armstrong demonstrates his coathanger trick.

97

THE RULES OF GOLF

OUTSIDE AGENCY

An 'outside agency' is any agency not part of the match or, in stroke play, not part of the competitor's side, and includes a referee, a marker, an observer or a forecaddie. Neither wind nor water is an outside agency. A bird or an animal which might disturb the ball is an outside agency.

ball will actually strike the body at exactly the same place, first on the backswing, then on the throughswing, on each swing. On both sides of the swing, it works. If the golfer is back on his heels, it will hit him lower. If he raises his head, or 'heightens' his swing in any way, the ball will swing around his neck and all but choke him.

All of Wally's gadgets make use of readily available, inexpensive items. One I particularly like in terms of its teaching effectiveness is the Sponge, a sponge shaped like a figure 8 and perhaps four inches thick. Held between the forearms just below the elbow, it is quite marvellous in keeping the elbows and arms in that fixed relationship which is essential, particularly on pitch shots. Tucked under the left armpit, it helps the left arm fold in on the follow-through and is very good in curing a slice. Many golfers let their left elbow float out towards the hole, away from their bodies on the follow-through, with dire effect on the ball flight. As the clubhead goes through the ball at impact and the right arm extends after it, the left elbow should fold in to the ribs and stay close to the body. Armstrong's sponge helps it do just that. Held between the knees, it will help develop footwork with practice swings going back and forth. Tucked between the right shoulder and the head, as though the head was being laid on a pillow, the sponge puts an end to the reverse pivot, that nasty habit golfers have of letting the weight go forward on to the left foot during the backswing, instead of easing most of it over to the right foot. All told, the Sponge, is an ingenious, multi-purpose golf aid, and another of Wally Armstrong's inspirations.

THE COURSE

BUILD ME A GOLF COURSE, MR ALLISS

In the early nineties, in spite of a severe recession throughout the western world, golf was booming. More and more people wanted to play, so more courses were needed to accommodate them. Indeed, in the autumn of 1992, in England alone, there were 206 18-hole golf courses listed as under construction. A report made by the R&A in 1989 had claimed that 700 courses would be needed to meet the demand. When a Conservative government in the eighties issued an edict to farmers that they could change the usage of their land, many farmers rushed off and got planning permission for golf courses, persuaded that the agricultural price of £1000 or £1500 per acre would become a golden £25 000 an acre for golf purposes, expecting to see developers come riding over the horizon with bags of gold, handing it out like confetti. And no more getting up at five o'clock on freezing winter mornings!

But the planners making such judgements at the time were surely being duped, or misguided. Dozens of applications were being granted without the slightest hope of their being put into effect. And perfectly valid schemes were being refused for what seemed idiotic reasons. In many cases, the Alliss/Clark golf design company has had a genuine developer, with the required capital, anxious to go ahead, only to be turned back by the relevant local authority because it has already used its full list of 'permissions'.

There is a rule, of course, that if you have not started construction within a certain period, even for a domestic garage, you must reapply. Nothing wrong with that, provided that the people who do reapply are told, when the circumstances demand it, 'Sorry, you didn't obey the rules.' So the R&A's 700 courses have much to contend with. And the recession has brought problems to the more glossy developments. At the proposed Loch Lomond Golf Club, near Luss, a course designed by Tom Weiskopf, with plans for a mansion house clubhouse, extensive property, time-share/marina and so on, the developers were stopped in their tracks by the recession. I haven't seen this site, but people whose opinion I respect say that it is magnificent. I do hope it will survive and prosper, but at five months long the season in Scotland is not as attractive as some people would like it to be.

Happily, the Loch Lomond Golf Club has been rescued to the extent that the Bank of Scotland, as I understand it, has arranged for the completion of the course and the provision of modified clubhouse facilities.

Several of these developments have reduced their prices, but sales of memberships have been dribbles and not the expected floods. If you are really brutal, location is the key – in business terms, very often there are not enough chimney pots. All golf courses, certainly in Scotland, need local memberships to sustain them twelve months of the year. Hotel, holiday makers, second-home people, the occasionals, will not do it. Not enough of them. Dornoch, for example, survives because it is 100 years old, it is famous, people are accustomed to making pilgrimages there, it's a lovely course, cost nothing to build, it's modest to maintain – it's wild, natural, like the courses in the West of Ireland. These good courses which have survived do so because they were built 100 years ago by Braid, Taylor and Old Tom Morris on ground that scarcely needed to be touched; they have become institutions. I exaggerate of course, but these places tiptoe along, with no great overheads, and they survive. In all of this, too many people have been greedy, and charged silly prices. There is still plenty of room for the right development in the right place at the right time.

Golf course architecture has come a long way in the last 30 years and there are changes still to come. In the old days, courses were built on natural land, cut through pine forests, laid out across heathland or along the shore. They were largely built by hand, with ploughs and drags and a few mules or horses dragging wagons in the background, all very different to the sophisticated earthmoving equipment available today. The research that has been done on the growing of grasses, the germination of seeds, different grass strains for different ground, temperature, overhead conditions, has made golf course design and construction a very big and interesting business. I have to smile when some of the established designers of the day from the 'amateur ranks' of golf lead off at the most alarming tangents at the fact that professional golfers are 'taking up' course design. What nonsense – go back in history and some of the finest courses ever designed were done by the early professionals, as far back as Old Tom Morris. Indeed the earliest of golf course architects were professionals or accidental amateurs who knew a bit about the game.

Sometimes it seems that golf architects are trying to outdo each other with bizarre designs. Jack Nicklaus, relatively new at the business, has created an enormous impression. Some people say that his courses – enormously expensive, very dramatic – are too difficult, designed only

Old Tom Morris. A portrait by Sir George Reid painted in 1903, five years before Tom died at the age of 87.

for golfers like himself who can hit a 2-iron 220 yards. There is a good deal of jealousy in all this. Jack is reputed to be involved in 50 to 60 courses at any one time, with a minimum fee of 1^1/_2$ million, so I can quite see that the green eye of jealousy would come into things. And the fact remains that his course designs are enormously successful.

I was lucky to have worked with Dave Thomas for nearly 25 years, creating some very well-known golf courses, and over the last six years I have been teamed with Clive Clark. Not many people know that Clive studied architecture for two years before becoming a professional golfer – 'real' architecture that was. We have created close to 20 courses throughout Europe, trying to combine style and character with playability. I sometimes think there ought to be prizes for golf architects, taking into account the budgets they have to work with. Some architects just do tees and greens and still take 10 per cent of the construction cost, which means they do very nicely. We like to think we are more imaginative, giving the client not only an interesting course but being able to offer a post-construction service, with PR and so on, and, of course, also finding the right staff – very important in today's world.

When I was younger, the most famous architect was Robert Trent Jones, the Welsh-born American who had a wonderful reputation for doing incredible things, particularly in moving soil and adding water. His course at Pevero in Sardinia is one of the most audacious I have ever seen. To take on the task of building a golf course over a mountain range, albeit with the Aga Khan as the client providing the necessary funds, was dramatic in the extreme. I always felt that Trent would have tackled a course halfway up Mount Everest if the budget was right.

The most outrageous designer today is the American, Pete Dye. At his Eagle Pines course in the Walt Disney World Resort, where we did our BBC filming, he maintains his reputation of being different. The course meanders through groves of pines, with lots of waterways, and instead of rough, Dye has carpeted the sides of his fairways with pine needles or 'pine straw' as the Americans call it. Thus Pete justifies his title as the Picasso of golf course design. Certainly he is a great innovator and, like most avant garde work, you can either like or dislike, but never ignore, what he does. The point of the pine needles surely is just to be different. The ball should sit on top of these needles. The difficulty I see for the average player, standing in two or three inches of pine needles, is that his feet are liable to move, and he is liable to hit behind the ball. So he has to make a very precise shot, a shot swept away, hit very cleanly. And he would have to be conscious of the hazards ahead, since from that surface, he would invariably be hitting a low scuttler. There is something of the same effect at Augusta, although the

The view from the secretary's office in the R&A clubhouse, St Andrews. Golfers leaving the first tee, the 18th green to the left.

pine needles are much more shallow, and are under the trees rather than lining the fairways.

Rumour has it that Pete Dye works with a staff of only two or three, including his wife (a talented golfer), and no doubt someone to answer the phone and do the letters. Pete apparently is moved to drive the bulldozer himself from time to time. He was one of the first of the modern architects to use railway sleepers, or 'railroad ties' American style, to sheer up the edges of tees or lakes or bunkers, an idea he got from Prestwick. For every superb course that he makes, he seems to design another which causes much controversy. 'The Teeth of the Dog' or La Romana in the Dominican Republic is quite spectacular, but then

103

the site was spectacular, running along the edge of the ocean, with little coves and inlets and waves pounding in excitingly.

There is a saying in the trade, rather a glib one, that if the site is good, a 10-year-old could design a course – just cut through the woods, go along the top of the cliff and you'd create something stunning. The real golf architect creates something acceptable out of a flat, 150-acre field, and a modest budget.

Pete Dye at Kiawah Island. Is that an evil glint in his eye?

One of Pete Dye's most famous courses is Kiawah Island, where the Ryder Cup was played in 1991. When I first saw it, I thought it dramatic indeed, and like most of Dye's work well worth a second glance. Of course, one had to take into account the fact that the environmentalists would not let him put the 18th hole where he wanted it, so the clubhouse couldn't go where he had wanted it. The thing became unbalanced – 9th green to 10th tee was about 600 yards, totally unacceptable you'd say, but of course riding on golf carts it would not make much difference.

Kiawah had three or four holes which were monstrously difficult, and perhaps two others that were farcical. The location by the ocean was wonderful, the way he handled the environment and the wildlife was striking. The environmentalists were so delighted that they said, 'Oh, go on, put the 18th where you wanted it.' Too late, too late was the fearsome cry, so that area became the practice ground.

One or two of the greens were perched up like giant mushrooms. With the wind off the sea at 20 or 30 mph, it was almost impossible to keep the ball on them. It was swept away, down the hill into a huge swale, like the Valley of Sin at St Andrews, but four times the size and three, four, five, six times as deep, if you can imagine it. And down there you were still on the putting surface. You couldn't see the bottom of the pin, so the thing was to give it a whack with the putter and hope for the best. The 17th hole, a par-3 entirely over water, was too long. The shot had to find a narrow green set across the line. There was nowhere else to go around the green. There were lots of modest disasters on the hole. Even the best players in the world are not that good. They don't have rifles in their hands. The vagaries of weather and ground, wind and bounce were more than many of the players could cope with. For all that, we had one of the most exciting of all the Ryder Cup matches, with only half a point or whatever between the teams.

The whole business of golf course design is fascinating. I wish club golfers showed more interest, not only in their own course and why a bunker is where it is and why it is the size it is, but in courses throughout the world, which are now shown on television. United States Open

Championship courses have been heavily criticized for their severity with each passing year, and they are different from what we are accustomed to. This is a generalization, and there are exceptions like Pebble Beach and Shinnecock Hills, but in the main they are cut through forests. Trees become a 'hazard' as well as bunkers and lakes. Scrub, heather, ferns, broom, gorse and the like which we experience are little known on these courses prepared by the United States Golf Association. The degree of difficulty in USGA courses is controlled by cultivating and grading the rough to a uniform thickness and length.

There will be a great overbearing canopy of trees through which narrow avenues are cut, and if you are off the fairway you are in deep rough and it is very punishing indeed. Often the USGA will allow a band of rough to grow across the front of greens so that the shot to the green must be flown all the way in the air. No possibility of running the ball on to these greens, and the USGA is being criticized increasingly for this sort of thing. On top of all this, the greens are hard and cut close, the whole thing compounded, and many players are concerned about this policy. The USGA attitude is that an Open Championship should be a severe test, but many people believe they go to extremes. And comparing such courses with the Masters at Augusta is like comparing chalk and cheese. At Augusta, you can be almost anywhere on the course and never lose a golf ball. If you are off the fairway and under trees, there is no rough and the lower branches are so high that you can usually get a swing and knock the ball back along the fairway. Not so in the US Open.

Comparing the US Open and our Open Championship is like comparing a Chinese meal with an Italian meal – can't be done. Both are excellent, but different. In the game's beginning here, conditions were wild and unkempt. Skilful players had to learn to be patient, to hold their temper, and work the ball round as best they could. Our championship courses are now very well groomed, but they are still links, exposed, with lots of bumps and bounces, sometimes true, sometimes not. But we don't seek to eliminate luck. That surely is part of the game's charm.

**A classic American parkland course –
the 6th hole at Oak Hill, Rochester
NY, where Curtis Strange won the
1989 US Open.**

THE CLUB

The game of golf has changed so much in my time that I find it very difficult to look at it clearly, objectively. I enjoyed the old club life, of leather armchairs and polished oak and brass; the smell of log fires and anthracite in the winter; copies of the *Daily Telegraph* and *The Times* and piles of old magazines, mainly *Golf Illustrated* and *Golf Monthly* since only they existed then. There was anchovy toast, crumpets dripping with butter, boiled eggs for tea. The club would be run by a fiery, eccentric colonel or wing commander, who as secretaries were both quite wonderful and frightening. They did command respect. Respect in the young seems to have gone. Forty years ago you never thought of cheeking a policeman or your teacher at school. You were terrified of swearing in public and anyone who did was a very bold character indeed. The game, in so many ways and like so much else of life today, has become homogenised.

The golf courses and clubhouses, in their designs, have not escaped this. Too much golf course architecture around the world has taken a lead from the kind of courses which have been demanded for American resort hotel developments, such as we had at the Walt Disney World Resort. Like the state of Florida itself, these are in the main flat. They have huge greens, necklaced by vast bunkers which are often more cosmetic than hazardous, and acres and acres of water. In hot climates, of course, this latter is important as reservoirs for watering systems or recycling purposes or for ecological reasons. Water too can have its cosmetic uses – at Augusta National, the club puts blue dye into its streams and lakes there during the Masters to make it look better on television, as though the course wasn't lovely enough. Modern golf developments, even in poor old Britain, seem to demand bigger and grander clubhouses. One of the grandest is Oaklands Hills in the Detroit area, where you might well find the boss of General Motors or the Ford Motor Company relaxing. There, the reception area is as lavish as any you would find in the swankiest London hotel, with huge vases of flowers everywhere, public rooms like railway termini – all wonderful and totally unnecessary.

Clive Clark and I have a modest dream that before I snuff it, we will build our own golf course and club, where people can really enjoy

(Above) Approaching the Clubhouse of the huge Oakland Hills Club near Detroit – one of the grandest golf developments in the world. (Left) The dining-room all dressed up for the President's Annual New Year Dinner.

the game of golf. Everything possible will be done for their pleasure, but they must behave and conform to our rules. If not, they will be considered disruptive, and removed. My ideal golf club would be a latter-day Swinley Forest, with staff who were an integral part of the whole thing. They would all play golf, and know the game. They would not be obsessed with wages, but they would be concerned with their quality of life, and with the quality of their labour, which would be second to none. They would rejoice in seeing the wildlife wandering about the putting green of a morning, provided it wasn't deer chewing the place up. They would be concerned above all with the betterment of the club, be respectful to members and be respected in return; never stepping over the line, in their own way they would be brimful of confidence and absolutely on top of the job. And they would at all times be looked after, in the way that the old 'aristos' looked after ghillies, caddies and artisans.

The fact is that there isn't really a 'snobbish' club in the British Isles. We have one or two which think they are superior, but compared to Augusta, Cypress Point or Burning Tree or a hundred other clubs in America, we don't have one here where you can't walk up the front drive and get into the clubhouse, or go into the pro shop or whatever. I speak to people who say, 'We are going to Atlanta, thought we might go over to Augusta and have a wander round and look at Augusta National.' I say, 'Oh no you won't – you won't get past the front gate on the front drive.' And they don't believe me, don't believe there are men in uniform with guns at the front gate, to keep you out. To us that seems quite ridiculous. At the Wack Wack Golf Club in Manila, there is a notice in the lobby saying, 'Members please check their guns with the receptionist'. People say, oh well, they're like that. It is not quite like that at Augusta, but it is not a million miles away from it.

The clubhouse at our 'ideal' golf club would be distinctive but modest, more than just functional but most of all not in any respect 'grand'. There are too many of these about in the new developments. It would have shower heads the size of dinner plates with a Niagara of hot water (the best in the world are surely at the Hong Kong Golf Club) – big, hot, steamy, with wooden pallets on the floor, disposable paper slippers, heaps of wonderfully absorbent towels, masses of talcum powder and other smellies. Delightful. The locker room would be the core room in my clubhouse. The one I saw at the Champions Club in Houston, Texas, where we played the Ryder Cup match in 1967, would be my ideal, on a smaller scale. The lockers would be of oak, spacious enough to take hangered clothing, and they would *not* be for golf bags. These would be stored elsewhere by the locker room staff,

gentlemen who would be on hand to clean shoes, serve drinks and sandwiches from the bar right there in the locker room, and in general mollycoddle the members. There would be round card tables with fresh packs of cards, a couple of television monitors on the wall – a man would scarcely need anything beyond the locker room. There would be a grill room upstairs, with a fixed menu of home-made soup, steak, hotpot, sandwiches, salad, hamburgers, that kind of thing, with a lunch service only. The clubhouse would close bang on nine o'clock in the summer, seven in the winter. The grill room I can imagine – red and white checked table cloths, condiment sets in the middle of the tables, two kinds of mustard, brown sauce and tomato sauce – terrific. No swimming pool, no tennis courts, no snobbish nonsense. But a practice ground, oh yes, there would be a practice ground.

Practice facilities in British golf are usually pretty thin on the ground. I cannot think of more than six clubs in Britain that have the practice facilities I have seen at dozens of clubs in the US. Why? It isn't always to do with weather. I think it is the remnant of the Victorian/Corinthian attitude that sport is for fun, that it should be learned by playing, and that there is something not quite proper about practising, as though by practising one is taking some kind of advantage

111

'THE MAN WHO MISSED THE BALL ON THE FIRST TEE AT ST. ANDREWS'   Cat. No. 3

over the other man. There are still remnants of the blimpish attitude of 'Good God, that fellow actually practises.' 'Never!' 'He does – turned up an hour before his tee-off time at last month's medal, chipping and putting, getting acclimatized to the weather. Pothunter!' Out, out, *out* !

We do have practice grounds that are big in area. Royal Birkdale, Turnberry and Hoylake come to mind. But when a championship comes along, even St Andrews struggles to find what by modern standards would be considered practice facilities. The Jack Nicklaus course at Muirfield Village has a most splendid practice ground. There are special pitching areas, deep bunkers and shallow bunkers for practising, chipping, practice greens of the same pace as those on the course. In our funny old country, the majority of clubs have either no or very poor facilities, an old decrepit net probably bought in the dim and distant past from a fisherman at Portland Bill. The club's big hitter could probably blast balls through it and the tarpaulin sheet behind, putting other members at risk. Most clubs could quite easily put up a couple of nets somewhere near the first tee so that members could have a few warm-up swings, if not sustained practice sessions. And often practice putting greens bear no relation to the speed and quality of the greens on the course. And there will be notices everywhere – 'No chipping to putting green', 'No chipping to 18th green'. But there is nowhere to practise chipping. A gloomy picture indeed. But it is all down to the members. If they insisted that part of their subscription went to just such basic facilities, things would certainly change.

THE PRO SHOP

8

When my brother and I took over Parkstone Golf Club back in the mid-fifties, we wanted to make an impressive start. After all, it was the first time we were to be head professionals. We packed the shop out with stock, between £1500 and £2000 worth. The secretary there at the time was J. D. Bond, known as 'Daddy' Bond. He said, 'Peter and Alec, you've gone over the top here, you'll never sell all this.' (We had some double-knit cashmere sweaters by Pringle, which we retailed for £4 10s – £4.50.) 'We just don't have the kind of members who can afford to buy sweaters like that.' I remember we did manage to clear them after a year or two.

The interesting thing was that Pringle was up for sale some years ago and could have been bought relatively cheaply. In the recent recession, thousands of people were laid off and paid off in the textile industry, with the Scottish Borders hard hit. Then along came Nick Faldo: tall, good-looking and striking, but above all winning golf championships wearing Pringle sweaters with designs that were most distinctive. It is said that Pringle provide £1 million of Faldo's very substantial annual income, that Pringle have had to take on extra labour, that sales were up 30 per cent in 1991 and were expected to be better in 1992. Certainly the Pringle shop at the 1992 Open Championship at Muirfield sold the goods just as fast as the factory could deliver them, and Faldo has been said to have 'saved Hawick'. Blarney or no, he has done tremendously well for them. I suspect that Pringle may be doing what 'Mr Ping' does with his golf clubs – make so many and when these are sold, it is 'wait for next year'. Perfectly good marketing.

The good thing as far as running a golf professional's shop back in my Parkstone days was that a sensible pro could live quite well on the turnover from the shop and a few lessons from the core of 40, 50 or 75 members who supported him. The slogan of the PGCA, the Professional Golfers' Cooperative Association, which was what its name implied and is no longer in existence, was 'Golfers who know, buy from their pro'. Not all golfers did that. Not all pros were worth supporting. But there was no poaching from other pros in the area. No advertising. There were no discount stores to undercut the professional with their volume turnover.

Nick Faldo, with his sponsor on his chest.

I sometimes think that too many people are taking too many bites at the cherry nowadays. There are just too many products. How well I remember my father and his contemporaries like the Whitcombe brothers, Henry Cotton and the rest of them, pottering around their shops, the smell of the glue pot simmering away in the back, the smell of leather as they re-gripped clubs, of tobacco and varnish, and the occasional cheeky words when a member came in with a not very good score. Henry Cotton was a figure grander than the rest of them, even from his earliest days. Golf shops in those days were poky places, carrying a few sets of clubs, golf balls and not a lot more. After the days of hickory, when members were always sniffing around, trying to find a club with a shaft which would match the clubs they already had, come the days of the matched sets of steel shafts, and pro shops in Britain gradually stocked more and more clubs. Over the past 20 years, that has gone into reverse, and the emphasis has been on clothing and other accessories. Pro shops have become retail palaces, with very few clubs to sell – and oh yes, a range of putters and drivers, magical clubs which will let you hole every putt and hit the ball 50 yards further.

Modern golf clubs and balls, like modern cars, are excellent. All the products are good. They make jokes about Lada cars, but they've all got windscreen washers, heaters and radios, and will go 300 miles on a tankful of petrol. The variety of merchandise in modern shops is extraordinary. I would not like the job of stocking a shop today because there must be 50 different shoe manufacturers. In my day, Lotus was the only one. Dunlop did make rubber shoes, but not until Saxone of Kilmarnock, a good old Scottish firm, started to make shoes in the early fifties (signing up Henry Cotton to wear them), was there any competition and some inroads made to the market. Now they flood in from America, Korea, Taiwan, everywhere.

Being a club professional now is a very different game from my time, and certainly my father's day. The modern shop, in your average town, might well have £50 000 of stock at any time. The better clubs, the Gleneagles-Turnberry-Wentworth-type clubs, would probably carry stock of more than £100 000. And there would be a need to turn that over three or four times in the year, what with wages to pay, VAT, general overheads – some clubs now want to charge a professional rent for the shop, something I never thought I would see. I should have thought most clubs would be happy to have their professional give them a tip-top service and make a decent living.

And the modern golf club professional needs to be rather more than a merchant. He has to know a good deal about the technology of golf clubs and golf balls, and talk of these matters to his members, some of

Bernard Gallacher and staff in his professional's shop at the Wentworth Club, one of the grandest in the UK.

whom may be world experts, face to face. Constant research and development, and the use of unfamiliar materials, have brought substantial changes to the game. The Japanese influence in 'high-tech' has been quite amazing. The Bridgestone 'Rextar' golf ball, launched at the 1992 Open Championship, had been put on test by such as Nick Faldo, Billy Ray Brown, Raymond Floyd and Mark Calcavecchia. They reported that they were not entirely happy with the flight of the ball. The Japanese scientists went away, dismantled the ball, stripped it to its basic components and did exhaustive tests to produce a golf ball that was as good as any that had ever, *ever* been made before!

Probably the greatest single change in golf equipment has happened to the golf ball, with the coming of the two-piece ball. It probably has been of the greatest advantage to the average golfer. It spins less. It does not hook so much, neither does it slice so much and, as a result, it flies slightly further. Where it loses is on control when it hits the green, but this is no hardship to the average golfer, who has very little control of the behaviour of his shots on to the putting surface. An even greater advantage to the average player is that these balls, with modern materials, are virtually indestructible.

Perimeter weighting is another development in clubheads which has been greatly publicized. It is again probably of more advantage to the average golfer rather than the expert. The movement of the weight of

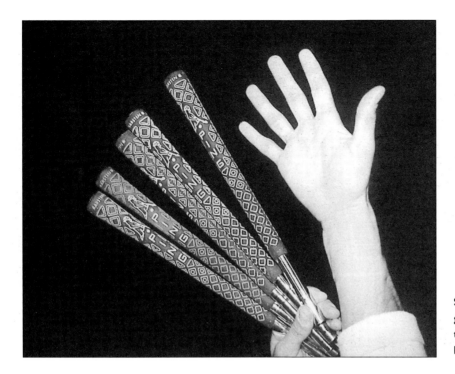

Shafts galore, clubs galore, but above all, the game still needs hands.

the clubhead to the perimeter, distributed round the edges with enough left in the centre to withstand the shock of the ball, means that the effect of a mis-hit shot will be substantially lessened. A ball hit off-centre with a traditionally weighted clubhead will be less effective, will go further astray, than a similar shot with a perimeter-weighted head. There have been remarkable advances in shaft manufacture, and in the materials used. The common objective has been to produce a shaft as strong as steel, but lighter, so that more weight can be placed in the clubhead. Shot for shot, more weight in the clubhead means that the ball can fly further.

Shafts are now made of graphite, carbon, titanium and other composite materials. People in the shaft business will baffle you with talk of weight, balance point, kickpoint, flex and torque. The club member does not have to know this – his club professional does, or at least the gist of it. The game is the same as it always has been – stand at the side, swing the clubhead, give the ball a whack and try to get it into a hole $4\frac{1}{2}$ inches across. Big Berthas, Jumbos, special heads, special shafts – do they do wondrous things for the golfer? Well, they do and they don't. When carbon-shafted clubs first came in, Tommy Horton and Hedley Muscroft tried them and improved their hitting distance by 30 yards. Other people said they didn't make the slightest difference. Rolls Royce almost went bust over carbon fibres. The Wilson Company put all its eggs in the aluminium-shafted basket. They made them 100 per cent of their output, and the whole thing died a death and cost them a great deal of money.

If it suits you, it suits you. That should be the criterion for the golfer in the pro shop. Remember, he'll always be prepared to let you test things. Golfers can certainly be sold equipment on the strength of what the game's star players do. When Jack Nicklaus won his last Masters using a putter with an outsize head, sales of the putter went rocketing in the next few weeks. The same was true of the driver with the huge head which John Daly wielded so dramatically in winning the 1991 US PGA Championship.

Over the history of the game, the manufacturers have always tried to improve. Always someone has tried to make a more sophisticated product. Golf balls were rough and ready, stitched together. Then gutta percha came in, still strips of rubber wound round, heated, moulded. So technology has always been on the move. Go to a motor museum, look at old cars, and wonder. The $4\frac{1}{2}$-litre Bentley is gorgeous, but changing gear in it and hauling it round corners must have been a labour of love. You wonder how people could sit in these old cars, much less drive them. Now you can hardly imagine anything more sophisticated than the modern car.

Of course, this is the age of the credit card, and it is quite common-place to be able to buy air tickets to New York and get there without spending any cash at all. But I do remember the shock I felt when I first heard the story of Gary Player travelling from Los Angeles to Johannesburg without having spent one cent in cash. The world is becoming so small, yet so full of computers and faxes and instant com-munications and more and more people wanting more and more goods and services, with everyone keen to appear perfect. The golf game is part of all this, the club professional is part of all this, and it is astonish-ing how it has grown in the past twenty years.

Manufacturers of clubs, balls, sweaters, shirts, clothing, caps, waterproofs, shoes, umbrellas — there was a time when the only golf umbrellas were 'Harlequins'. I'd really like to know who was the first person to put a logo on a golf umbrella or on a golf bag. In my time, nobody had logos. I remember Peter Thomson saying, when Pringle first brought out their little lion logo, that he wasn't going around 'advertising other people's clothing' — he used to cut labels *off* clothing. Very different today with Ian Woosnam going around with patches on his shirt extolling the virtues of manufacturers' products — more and more like Grand Prix drivers every day.

ADVICE FROM ALLISS

WINTER GOLF

We filmed *So You Want to Play Golf* in Florida in the winter, with the sun shining and shirt sleeves the order of the day. It was hard to believe that all over northern Europe tens of thousands of golfers were striving to play golf, if not every day, then every weekend throughout the winter – wrapped around with scarves, gloves woolly hats and waterproofs. But lots of people do play golf throughout the winter months and, if you prepare for it properly, you can get a great deal of enjoyment out of it. Too many people rush out on to the course in winter, ill-prepared, and expect too much.

One of the great basics is – you must always be warm. A pair of big mittens, easy slip-ons, slip-offs, is always a very good thing to have. Not mittens alone, but there is a very good gadget, rather like a tea bag which, when you unwrap it and rub, rub, rub it warms up and stays warm for four or five hours. One of these inside the mitten keeps your hand warm, and that in turn will certainly help you play better golf. If the 'extremities' are covered and warm, that helps a lot. So shoes – make sure they are waterproof. Not many UK courses, for example, drain well in winter, and feet that are less than dry and snug are a distraction and an irritation.

I think it is sensible, especially as we grow older, to have our heads covered in cold wet weather. A hat, cap, woollie, whatever, is recommended – so much of the heat loss goes through the roof!

A decent golf suit, waterproof and windproof, is essential. Anything less than a good quality suit is false economy. They tear, they sweat, they don't do a lot of good, but if you buy a good quality suit, then of course you must look after it. The same is particularly true of shoes. How often we've known people spend a couple of hundred pounds in the pro shop, get the shoes and waterproofs wet, bung them in the back of the car with the umbrella, never to be seen for a week, then the owner going back to the poor old pro and complains that these shoes-umbrellas-golfsuit have lasted only five minutes or so!

Another thing about winter golf, and something which I think is sadly neglected in many parts of the country, is why foursome golf is not played more often – two balls, four players. It gets you round

Ready for anything October weather at St Andrews can bring. Fred Couples of the US team, Alfred Dunhill Cup, 1992.

THE RULES OF GOLF

'WINTER RULES'

As far as the Rules of Golf are concerned, there is no such thing. The words do not appear in the rules. Neither, incidentally, does the word 'fairway', which will surprise lots of people.

However in an appendix to the rules, Appendix 1, it makes clear that a club committee can make a temporary local rule to cover abnormal conditions. The reference in the appendix is 4 (b) in which, under such a temporary local rule, the committee will allow you to roll the ball over into a better lie, usually within six inches of where it lay, or lifted out of its own plug mark. At the same time it is permitted to clean the ball. All of this is designed to 'protect the course or promote fair and pleasant play'.

quicker, it is good exercise, it is very competitive and the alternate shotmaking means you think a great deal more about the game, and about your swing, because you don't want to put your partner into a troublesome place.

Winter golf should really be treated as a nice walk, and good excuse for some exercise, and lots of fresh air. Lots of times there will be temporary tees, temporary greens, rolling the ball over on the fairway. You mustn't expect to play your best golf in these winter months, but the game can be very enjoyable indeed if you go about it the right way. But if it is pouring with rain, leave it alone. Forget it. Rain gets in everywhere, and keeping dry, pulling a trolley, wrestling with an umbrella — it just isn't worth it. Stay in the clubhouse. It has its pleasures too, you know.

Bobby Locke, one of the great champions before the First World War, shows slender style.

SLOW PLAY

Slow play is one of the curses of modern golf. Many reasons have been put forward as to why play should have slowed so dramatically over the past 10 or 15 years. Perhaps it's because we have so many new players coming in who have not been schooled by the old, retired wing commanders and colonels who were club secretaries in my day, and took control of these things. This is a pity. These 'nouveau' golfers are missing quite a lot and they could get much more out of the game. Certainly the people playing behind them could get more fun out of it!

Some players don't take the precaution, the simple precaution, of having a spare ball in a pocket. So if they lose a ball and spend time searching around in the rough, they have to walk back 30, 40, 50 yards to their golf bag to get another, and perhaps do it all over again! Some of them never even have a tee peg in their pockets. When it is their time to play, the glove isn't on, so there is the business of putting it on before they can take up a grip and stance. Just imagine the time it takes to extract a glove from your back pocket, perhaps on a rather sticky day, squeeze your fingers in it, flex them, fasten the glove, then step up to the ball and find you don't have a tee peg handy. That means another dive into the golf bag. So you waste 20, 30, 40 seconds, and you do this on every hole, on virtually every shot and you are playing fourball – at the end of all that the round can be an hour, an hour and a half, longer than it need be.

The Rules of Golf say, 'In the interests of all, players should play without undue delay.' This is a problem, since no one can say what undue delay might be. Playing in the steaming heat of Thailand or the thin air of Mexico City, getting round in three hours might be unreasonable, or even impossible. The weather, other golfers on the course, can affect the pace, but in the temperate UK three hours for a round should be within the powers of most golfers.

Everyone in your group should follow the flight of every shot – then the chances of one in the rough being found are heightened. The rules say that you have five minutes to find such a ball – don't make the people playing behind wait that long. Let them through, if the hole ahead is clear. Give some thought to your next shot as you are approaching your ball, not just when you reach it. On the green the player furthest from the hole will play first, and if that is not you, then you have a chance to study your line, and be ready to putt as soon as your turn comes. Too much time is wasted by people fooling around on greens. When all putting is finished and the flagstick replaced, everyone should get off the green, smartly.

But we can't blame handicap golfers for all the slow play. In the

Tournament pile-up on the 2nd tee at Wentworth, with at least five golf bags showing.

world of professional golf, in the World Cup for instance, when teams of two players represent each country, players have been known to take six hours 45 minutes to complete a round. On a hot and humid day, that is no fun. At the lovely Magnolia course at the Walt Disney World Resort, there is a sign on the tee saying '15 minutes per hole please, so that everyone can enjoy it. Thank you!' They allow you four and a half hours there, somewhat of an improvement on the fourball professional game. But at the Trevose club in north Cornwall, there is a sign on the first tee which insists 'Three hours is too long for 18 holes'. In this day and age, that might be a bit quick, but I know which philosophy I prefer.

The irony is that in my day Bobby Locke, the great South African champion, was constantly castigated for playing slowly. Locke would perambulate, rather than walk, round the course. He always played before huge crowds, crowds which in those days walked the fairway. Locke would take two and three-quarter hours, perhaps two hours 50 minutes, to play a round. That was a single, of course, a two-ball match, but Locke then was averaging 45 minutes quicker than the briskest of them today. And he had to get through the spectators, on every second shot, on to every tee, on to every green. A nightmare for the man. Locke never spent undue time over the shot. He had that well decided as he walked up to the ball.

We don't have to be sprinters, but we should also not be sluggards.

CORPORATE GOLF

The 12th green of the St George's Course on the island paradise of Bermuda.

If you had asked me twenty years ago whether I could ever imagine that I would live to see the day when someone would have an air shot, a stone cold miss, on the first tee of the King's Course at Gleneagles Hotel, or on the first tee at Sunningdale, Wentworth or St Andrews, I would have said, 'Rubbish – can't possibly happen.' Well, it does. Corporate golf has made it happen.

Corporate golf has become huge business over the past 10 or 15 years. In a way, that is a compliment to the game: business companies have been attracted by the image of golf, the fact that it is played all across society, in a thoroughly pleasant environment, beautiful places, and the people in the game (the administrators at national and club level, their staffs, the media, the tournament and club professionals) all behave in a rational manner. So too, in the main, do the spectators. There are the odd lapses in behaviour, but golf is a game which is hooligan-free. Many companies have come to see the game as a vehicle for giving bonuses, incentives or rewards, to staff. Off they go, the favoured ones, on golfing holidays to all corners of the world, or rather to the comfortable corners of the world, such as the Mediterranean coast or Florida or Bermuda. Often the families will go too, and while dad is playing golf and having a few three-putts, mum and the children can enjoy the beach, the sunshine, Disney World, whatever. Some companies may even have their own golf societies, which produce another side to the same coin. Two or three times a year these societies will have a day's golf at a course of their choice, and this aspect of the game has 'saved' many golf clubs in the sense that it has provided a large slice of their income. Even back in the sixties, a club like Wentworth was collecting 40 per cent of its income from visiting golf societies.

Roughing it (?) as a modern golf championship spectator.

There is another element to corporate golf which is the company entertainment pavilion at a major event, the Open Championship being the outstanding example. In September 1992, the R&A gave notice of their prices for 'corporate hospitality' at the Open Championship of 1993, under two separate headings. First was the 'Private Chalet', second was the 'Executive Restaurant'.

The 'Private Chalet', of 80 square metres, would be one of a terrace of the most sophisticated tentage, with a covered entrance and outside patio, boasting an external company nameboard and a pole for the company flag. It would be floored, carpeted, decorated. The contract would provide 200 admission tickets (50 per day), 100 car-parking passes (25 per day), morning coffee and pastries, four-course luncheon with silver service, afternoon tea and cakes, two reserved grandstand seats at the 18th green, private telephone facilities, closed-circuit television coverage, and 30 official programmes and draw sheets delivered each day to the chalet. Price? £26 500! Now after you've taken a deep breath and said, 'Monstrous, disgraceful' and so on, just think of that price on a per capita basis. For 200 people, it amounts to £132.50 each – not such bad value if you think that a day's golf for a society, or a company day at Wentworth or a golf club of similar status, will run to around £100, and you will not be seeing the Open Championship. On that basis, and without even considering the price of a ticket for the opera, it becomes much more competitive.

The Executive Restaurants at Royal St George's, where the 1993 Championship was scheduled, were aimed at companies which did not require a pavilion exclusively, but which wanted to entertain a mini-

mum of eight or a maximum of 30, guests each day. Prices were to range from £140 to £155 per person per day. This price provided the same services as a pavilion, with an admission ticket for each guest, a parking pass per two guests. And all of this, pavilions and restaurants, was about as close as could be to the action – the tented village at Royal St George's is always set up alongside the first fairway.

People who do not attend the Open would find it difficult to comprehend the tremendous atmosphere which it generates, or just how

huge an event it is, requiring several thousand people to put it together and service it. And if these prices and the financial figures the championship deals in seem frightening, it has to be remembered that the R&A exists in a commercial and competitive world, and clearly they are obliged to have the championship generate as much surplus as possible, not only to maintain its standards but because much of that surplus filters down throughout the entire world of golf, with grants being given in a multitude of directions for the benefit of the game at large.

In September 1992, the R&A announced that the 1993 Cham-

The Red Arrows give the nod to the end of a great occasion at St Andrews, with the gallery packed around the 18th green.

pionship would have prize money of £1 million for the first time, and first prize would be £100 000. The winner's compensation may have seemed more than ample, but it still leaves the tournament golfer a long way behind other professional sportsmen such as tennis players, Grand Prix drivers and jockeys, not to mention American footballers and basketball and baseball players. Sustaining this prize money increase are increased admission charges, now up to £20 any one of the four championship days, though the R&A offers various discount arrangements for advance ticket sales.

An overview of the Hazeltine Club and the US Open of 1991 – championship golf just gets bigger and bigger.

Surely this, and the fact that admission to something like the 1993 Ryder Cup matches is now as high as £35 per day, puts the R&A Executive Restaurants and Private Chalets into the right kind of perspective.

There is another side to the coin, of course, and one rather disappointing aspect of all this is that in golf, as in tennis and cricket now, there is apt to be a block of grandstand seats in prime position standing empty almost all day. These are corporate guest seats, liable to be filled only on the last day, or only to see the leaders of the event come in, or in these other sports which have copied the example of golf, at the very climax of the event.

The way these tented villages have been laid out, copied I should say by the US Open, is quite brilliant, a masterpiece of planning. When you consider power, light, drainage, grandstands, telephones and general communications, catering, supply and servicing and clearance, all of it temporary, all of it outdoors, it is all quite splendid. What would Harry Vardon and Jimmy Braid, and why, Old Tom Morris, make of it all. . .?

From the corporate point of view, when a company can entertain guests or staff or important clients, what better place than a Gleneagles, a Turnberry, a Sunningdale? And corporate golf has introduced many people to the game. Perhaps it has tempted many guests to declare themselves golfers, the kind that is who play twice a year and have no real idea of the etiquette of the game, or its rhythms and balances, or the basics of the golf swing. That is why I have come across air shots on the first tee at Gleneagles and Sunningdale and Wentworth. Letting some corporate guests loose on these courses is like giving a 15-year-old the keys to a Ferrari and saying, 'Go ahead, drive it.' I suppose one can't blame the poor dear petals. If they haven't been told how, they can't be expected to do it right.

Corporate golf has become enormous. It has changed the face of golf as much as the Ping club or the two-piece ball or Japanese technology. It is here to stay. No doubt it needs to be harnessed to some extent, but it is splendid – certainly for the company guests!

Morning dew on the Magnolia course at Disney World, and the start of another round – who could ask for anything more?

INDEX